Ministry in the Spirit

The *Sword of the Spirit* series:

www.swordofthespirit.co.uk

Copyright © 2007, 1997 by Colin Dye
Second edition

Kensington Temple
KT Summit House
100 Hanger Lane
London, W5 1EZ

Scriptural quotations, unless otherwise stated, are from the New King James Version. Thomas Nelson Inc. 1991.

Sword of the Spirit

Ministry in the Spirit

Colin Dye

Contents

Introduction

There is something of God's compassion in all humanity. No matter how distant a person may be from God, there are very few men and women who are not moved by the painful images they see in the media of lives which have been crushed by some new disaster. We do not need to know an individual personally to empathise with their suffering and to wish that we could do something to help them.

Close at hand, most people know somebody who is troubled by illness or accident, by unemployment, debt or family breakdown, by social isolation, some form of evil or just the stress of modern-day life. As Christian believers, we find that our human compassion is greatly intensified by the Holy Spirit, and we long to reach out to the bruised lives around us, and to help them receive God's comfort and counsel.

Of course, we should pray for the hurting people we know – pleading with God to intervene in their lives and bring his transforming wholeness. But, deep down, we know that we should be doing something ourselves; that we should be acting and speaking in a way which makes a genuine lasting difference.

As Christian believers, we are part of Christ's body on earth. We are Jesus' hands and voice in the world; and he has anointed us with his Holy Spirit so that – through us – he can do today for many in our nations what he did himself when he was on this earth. And this is precisely the mandate he has given us. He sends us out as his representatives to preach the gospel, heal the sick, cast out demons and to serve the world. He calls us to make disciples of all nations and to teach people through our words and deeds to follow Christ. This is the true work of the Church and it is only possible through the power of the Holy Spirit.

Acts 10:38 describes how God anointed Jesus with the Holy Spirit and power, and how he went about doing good and healing all who were oppressed by the devil – because God was with him.

As we live in partnership with the Spirit, and are moved, motivated and empowered by him, so we too can speak God's words, can carry out his deeds, can do his good, can pass on his healing to those who are oppressed by the evil one, and can offer God's help to some of the hurting people around us. This is true ministry in the Spirit.

This book is essentially for those believers who will set aside their own ideas about helping people, and will study God's Word to discover God's revelation about ministering in and with the Spirit.

There is additional material available to facilitate your learning, which can be found in the respective *Sword of the Spirit Student's Handbook* and on the website *www.swordofthespirit.co.uk*. In the handbook there is a complimentary study guide for each chapter, along with *Discussion questions* and *Quick quizzes*. After signing up for this module on the website, you will be able to access more quizzes and exams. There is also a *Webtool* (the book text with embedded links to bible references), and comprehensive audio and video teaching. Using these additional materials will help you test, retain and apply the knowledge you have learnt in this book.

You will also be able to use the *Student's Handbook* with small groups. You may wish to prayerfully select those parts that you think are most relevant for your group. This would mean that at some meetings you might use all the material whilst at others you might use only a small part. Please use your common sense and spiritual insight. Please feel free to photocopy these pages and distribute them to any group you are leading.

By the time you have finished working through this volume, it is my prayer that you will understand how God wants you to be willing to deal with demons, how he expects you to be ready to heal the broken-hearted, how he intends to do good through you – and that you will be eager to respond to his prompting.

Colin Dye

Ministry in the Spirit

Part One

Ministry in the Spirit

'Ministry' is one of the most commonly used words in the church today. We describe particular men and women as 'ministers', we talk about people 'ministering' and we refer to 'the ministry'. Each group of Christian believers normally knows what it means by these words, but other church groups often have a different understanding.

Some traditions, for example, reserve the word 'minister' for full-time, fully-paid leaders, while others use it more widely. Equally, a few churches use 'ministry' to identify the part of a meeting when they pray with people, while several use it as a general term for ministers' work.

What is ministry?

In studying *Ministry in the Spirit*, it is important that we begin by understanding what the Bible means by 'ministry'. There are three main groups of Greek words in the New Testament which are translated into English in the same way. Each word-group has a distinctive meaning, and we grasp the biblical significance of 'ministry' by appreciating the breadth of meaning passed on by all the words.

1. *Diakonos*

Diakonos is the Greek word for an ordinary, private house-servant. It was used to describe someone who swept their employer's floor, prepared food, served at tables, washed dishes, and so on. *Diakonos* is translated as 'minister' in Romans 13:4; 15:8; 1 Corinthians 3:5; 2 Corinthians 3:6; 6:4; 11:15; Galatians 2:17; Ephesians 6:21; Colossians 1:7, 23, 25; 4:7; 1 Thessalonians 3:2 & 1 Timothy 4:6. In some Bibles, it is translated as 'attendant' or 'deacon', but it always carries an association with a private house-servant.

Diakoneo, 'to serve', is usually translated as 'to minister'. Again, the Greek word for cleaning the floor and preparing food is used for spiritual activity in Matthew 20:28; 25:44; 27:55; Acts 19:22; Romans 15:25; 2 Corinthians 3:3; 2 Timothy 1:18; Philemon 1:13; Hebrews 6:10; 1 Peter 1:12 & 4:10–11. *Diakoneo* suggests that we should have a humble attitude towards ourselves and our service or ministry.

Diakonia, 'serving', is the main New Testament word for 'ministry'. Luke 10:39–41 illustrates its ordinary meaning of domestic duties, but it is commonly used to suggest spiritual service. It is used to describe:

◆ Apostles – Acts 1:17, 25; 6:4; 12:25; 21:19 & Romans 11:13

◆ Believers – Acts 6:1; 11:29; Romans 12:7; 15:31; 1 Corinthians 16:15; 2 Corinthians 8:4; 9:1, 12; Ephesians 4:12 & 2 Timothy 4:11

◆ The Holy Spirit – 2 Corinthians 3:8–9

◆ Angels – Hebrews 1:14

◆ Preachers and teachers – Acts 20:24; 2 Corinthians 4:1; 6:3; 11:8; 1 Timothy 1:12; 2 Timothy 4:5 & Colossians 4:17.

The *diakonos* word-group shows that 'a minister' is not a master, that 'to minister' does not mean 'to command', and that 'the ministry' is not a high office or a high status activity. In thinking biblically about 'ministry', we must begin by grasping that 'a minister' is rather like a low status domestic servant, and that 'ministry' is work similar to cleaning, car maintenance and cooking. This may seem surprising, for all too often we falsely see ministry as the domain of the spiritually elite.

2. *Leitourgos*

Leitourgos is occasionally used in the New Testament to identify 'a minister', but it carries a completely different meaning to *diakonos*. *Leitourgos* is the Greek word for an important public servant, for someone who carries out a public office at their own expense.

Diakonia describes full-time, low status, low paid, private serving by someone who is directed by their employer; whereas *leitourgia* refers to part-time, high status, unpaid, public service. In the New Testament, *leitourgos*, 'a minister'; *leitourgeo*, 'to minister'; and *leitourgia*, 'ministry', are used to describe:

- ◆ Christ – Hebrews 8:2
- ◆ Paul – Romans 15:16
- ◆ Epaphroditus – Philippians 2:25
- ◆ Prophets and teachers at Antioch – Acts 13:2
- ◆ The duty of the Gentile churches towards poor Jewish believers – Romans 15:27
- ◆ The practical responsibilities of believers towards each other – 2 Corinthians 9:12 & Philippians 2:17–20.

The New Testament uses *leitourgos* to describe Christian ministry much less frequently than *diakonos*, yet the 'high status' idea associated with *leitourgos* often dominates modern Christian thinking about ministry. The New Testament emphasis shows that a biblical understanding of ministers and ministry should be based in *diakonos*, and that we should think of ministry primarily as an ordinary, private, everyday, 'serving' activity.

The occasional use of *leitourgos*, however, underlines the fact that we do not serve for our own benefit, and it reminds us that ministry is important, can be public, and has a representative character.

3. *Huperetes*
The Greek word *huperetes* is translated in many versions of the Bible as 'minister'. It literally means an 'under-rower' and was used in New Testament times as a popular or colloquial word for any subordinate who acted under the direction of another person.

Huperetes, and *hupereteo* 'to minister or serve', are used in the New Testament to describe:

- ◆ A synagogue attendant – Luke 4:20
- ◆ Mark – Acts 13:15

♦   King David – Acts 13:36
♦   Paul – Acts 20:34; 26:16 & 1 Corinthians 4:1.

The use of *huperetes* stresses that ministers are not people who are in charge of their own activities, they are men and women who function under authority. Acts 13:36 shows that the great King David was only an 'under-rower' of God, and 1 Corinthians 4:1 states that first century church leaders should be considered and treated as 'under-rowers' – as people under the leadership and direction of Christ.

Service

When we take these three word-groups together, we can appreciate that scriptural ministry means service and that a biblical minister is a servant. We can say that, in general, the New Testament uses *diakonos* to show the link between ministers and their serving work, *leitourgos* to emphasise the representative nature of their service, and *huperetes* to stress their serving relationship with their superior, with Christ.

Perhaps the simplest and most accurate way we can think biblically about ministry is by replacing it with the word 'serving'. The basic message of the New Testament is that 'a minister' is always 'a servant', that 'to minister' is always 'to serve', and that 'ministry' is always 'service'. Any idea or pattern or practice of ministry which moves away from humble servanthood is not rooted in the Scriptures.

Slaves and hired servants

While we must remember that a biblical minister is always a servant, we must also realise that every biblical reference to a servant does not refer to a minister. Two Greek word-groups are used in the New Testament to describe 'servants' but are not translated as 'ministers'.

Doulos is the most common Greek word for servant and signifies a servant who is owned by his master in contrast to one who is employed by his master. In New Testament times, *doulos* referred to a slave. The main difference between *doulos* and *diakonos* is that *doulos* points to a relationship whereas *diakonos* indicates an activity.

Doulos is used in the New Testament to show that believers are owned and controlled by God. We see this in Romans 1:1; Galatians 1:10; Ephesians 6:6; Philippians 1:1; Titus 1:1; James 1:1; 1 Peter 2:16; 2 Peter 1:1 & Jude 1:1. Because we are owned by God, we are called:

- ◆ To serve God – Matthew 6:24; Romans 7:6 & Philippians 2:22
- ◆ To serve Christ – Acts 20:19; Romans 12:11; 14:18; 16:18; Ephesians 6:7 & Colossians 3:24
- ◆ To serve one another – Galatians 5:13.

Slaves must obey their masters, so *doulos* points to the way we serve because we are owned by God. Servants also have to be obedient to their employers, but an element of willingness is inherent to *diakonos* – public servants are volunteers and private servants can stop working for their employer whenever they want to. It is this willingness which sets *diakonia*, 'ministry', apart from *doulos*, 'service'. We can say that a minister is someone who willingly makes themselves available to God to serve him in any way that he chooses.

Latris is the second word for 'servant' not translated as 'minister'. *Latris* literally means 'a hired servant' and *latreuo*, 'to serve', is used in the New Testament to describe the particular spiritual service of the priests and Levites who were paid to serve God in the temple, and the worship which believers offer God. We see this in Luke 1:74; 2:37; Acts 7:7; 24:14; 27:23; Romans 9:4; 12:1; Hebrews 9:1 & 14.

We should note that the New Testament uses priestly language about the body of believers rather than any individual believers. This means that *latris* service is corporate rather than individual. The New Testament makes it clear that all believers are called to serve/worship God like the priests and Levites with prayer, praise, thanksgiving and spiritual sacrifices.

But, unlike the priests and Levites, the Scriptures do not encourage us to expect to be paid for this work.

We are not called to be *latris* – hired servants who work primarily for the pay. Instead, we are called to be *diakonos* – willing servants who carry on serving because we love our employer and his household, and who are always volunteering for extra service.

The pattern of ministry

Matthew 20:28, Mark 10:45 & John 13:1–17 make it clear that Jesus came to give service not to receive service, to serve rather than to be served, to minister rather than to be ministered to.

These verses were a revolutionary statement which turned Daniel 7:13–14 upside down. The Jews were expecting that the Son of Man would be served by all people, nations and languages. Jesus claimed to be, and was, that Son of Man, but he made it plain that his everlasting kingdom would be led by a servant and characterised by service.

It is important to recognise that *diakoneo*, not *leitourgeo*, is the word used in Matthew 20:28 & Mark 10:45. This shows that:

◆ Private, lowly 'domestic' service is the foundation, pattern and style of Jesus' ministry, and therefore of all true Christian ministry

◆ It is possible for everyone to minister.

If *leitourgeo* had been used in these verses, it would have suggested that only special people could minister like Jesus. It should be plain that, as his service is *diakoneo*, we can all minister like him.

It is very significant that *diakoneo* is also used in Acts 6:2. This is the first recorded example of the church appointing people to minister, and the purpose of their ministry is 'serving tables'.

It is equally important to recognise that, two verses later, *diakonia* is also used to describe the apostles' service or ministry of the word. This emphasises that there is no difference between so-called 'practical' ministry and 'spiritual' ministry. Serving at tables is as much a part of Christ-like *diakonia* ministry as teaching God's Word.

Whenever we minister or serve, whether by polishing pews or preaching sermons, we should follow the pattern and example of Christ who humbly and lovingly served all people. We can see this pattern throughout the New Testament:

- ◆ Angels minister to Jesus – Matthew 4:11 & Mark 1:13
- ◆ Women minister to Jesus – Matthew 27:55 & Luke 8:3
- ◆ Jesus is ministered to in the person of the needy – Matthew 25:44
- ◆ Believers minister to each other – Romans 15:25; 1 Corinthians 16:15; 2 Corinthians 8:4; 9:1; Hebrews 6:10 & 1 Peter 4:10
- ◆ Ministry helps to reveal the gospel – 1 Peter 1:12
- ◆ Ministry helps to accomplish reconciliation – 2 Corinthians 5:18
- ◆ The ability to minister is a gift of God – Acts 20:24; Colossians 4:17; 1 Timothy 1:12; 1 Peter 4:11 & Romans 12:7.

A spiritual gift

The inclusion of ministry, *diakonia*, in the Romans 12:3–8 list of spiritual gifts helps us to understand that ministry is a gift rather than a duty, and that it comes from God rather than from within ourselves.

By placing ministry alongside prophecy, teaching, preaching, giving, leading and showing mercy, Paul also reveals that 'ministry' is as distinct from the other Romans 12 gifts as 'prophecy' is from 'showing mercy' and 'leading' is from 'giving'.

Modern believers sometimes ask who will be ministering at a meeting, when they really want to know who will be preaching. Romans 12:3–8 suggests that we should understand ministry – serving – in a much wider way.

Ephesians 4:7–16 is another passage about Christ-enabled gifts, and ministry, *diakonia*, is mentioned again. Verses 10 & 11 state that apostles, prophets, evangelists, pastors and teachers are gifts of the ascended Christ to the Church; and verse 12 reveals their purpose. They have been given so that all the saints – all God's people – are equipped for the work of ministry, for the building up of Christ's body.

This suggests four principles about *diakonia*, ministry or serving:

hand Book
P12

- ◆ It is more the work of ordinary saints than of apostles, pastors, prophets and teachers. Leaders are supposed to equip the saints to minister, they are not meant to do it for them.

- ◆ It is the purpose of saints. Just as Jesus came to serve, *diakonia*, so saints are equipped by leaders primarily to minister, *diakonia*.

- ◆ It is distinct from the teaching, prophesying, pastoring, training carried out by the leaders.

- ◆ It is a general expression, a generic term, for the whole work of Christian service. Just as a domestic servant could be asked to carry out any household duty and it would all be called service, so all acts of obedient Christian service can be considered as ministry.

1 Corinthians 12:1–11 is a third New Testament passage about spiritual gifts, and we should not be surprised to find that *diakonia* is mentioned again. Verses 4–6 follow a trinitarian structure and state that there are different gifts, but the same Spirit; different ministries, but the same Lord; different activities or workings, but the same God. This underlines that true ministry is rooted in Jesus. All genuine ministry is based in him, for we are called to minister as he ministered. He is the only pattern, foundation and source for all Christian ministry.

I Corinthians 12:4–6 also suggests that 'ministries' which come from the Lord are very closely related to 'gifts' from the Spirit and 'activities' from God. Verses 8–10 are traditionally thought of as 'gifts of the Spirit', but the preceding verses imply that it is equally valid to consider them 'ministries of the Lord' and 'activities of God'.

In Part Three of *Knowing the Spirit* we examine Jesus' earthly ministry, see him using many different gifts of the Spirit, and note how he helps us to minister through the gifts. In Part Seven of *Knowing the Spirit*, we study spiritual gifts and see that they are tools which enable us to get on with the task of glorifying Christ in the world, and that they are supernatural manifestations which the Spirit makes available to all believers so that the kingdom of God can be promoted.

This means, first, that the gifts of wisdom, knowledge, faith, healings, miracles, prophecy, discerning of spirits, tongues and interpretation are given to help us to minister as Jesus ministered; and second, that our understanding of ministry must be thoroughly charismatic – our service must be 'in the Spirit' if it is to be genuine scriptural ministry.

This *Sword of the Spirit* volume may be entitled *Ministry in the Spirit*, but this should not be taken to suggest that there can be true ministry which is not 'in the Spirit'. Everything that Jesus did was motivated, directed and empowered by the Spirit; his teaching, his praying and his serving was always fully 'in the Spirit'.

It is the same for us. It does not matter whether our service is spiritual or practical, whether it involves distributing food or casting out demons, it must be energised and directed by the Spirit. If it is to be effective, every single act of Christian service must be 'in the Spirit'.

We have seen that, in Acts 6:2, *diakoneo* is used to describe the practical serving work which needed to be done by the first ministers. The following verses, 3–7, report how the people chosen for this work had to be 'full of the Spirit'. Although their ministry was primarily administrative and practical, it was vital that it would be 'in the Spirit'.

General and particular

In this first Part, we have tried to establish a biblical overview of ministry in the Spirit. In the rest of this volume, we first examine some general biblical principles of all ministry, and then study several different aspects of scriptural ministry in the Spirit.

We have seen that ministry is a general, 'catch-all' expression for every way that we serve God and each other. This means that the material we will cover is bound to be selective and far from exhaustive – for nobody could examine every possible way that we can minister.

The following Parts are rooted in the ministry of Jesus. They describe the Old Testament basis and the New Testament record of his different serving activities, and set out the wider biblical principles which relate to those activities. This means that we will study the way Jesus healed, blessed, counselled and set people free from evil powers. Although we will not study any special examples, we must not forget that he also served people by feeding and washing them.

We have noted that the New Testament does not make a distinction between spiritual and practical service, but we have also established that Romans 12 distinguishes 'ministry' from activities like 'preaching' and 'prophesying'. This creates a problem for some believers. They recall that Acts 6 describes the apostles' service of the Word as 'ministry' and wonder, therefore, why Romans 12 distinguishes ministry from preaching. They ask how the apostles' preaching can both be ministry and be distinguished from ministry.

The simple answer is that the Bible often uses a word in a large and a small way – *generally* and *particularly*. Prophecy, for example, can be used to describe all speaking inspired by the Spirit: this way, much preaching can be considered prophetic. Yet prophecy can also be used in a more restricted way to refer to special messages from God which are spoken to particular individuals. It is not inaccurate to identify some preaching as prophetic, we merely need to make it clear whether we are using the word 'prophecy' in a *general* or a *particular* sense.

It is the same with ministry. We can think about the word both for 'every way that we serve', and also for 'particular personal serving activities'. Used generally, 'ministry' refers to every serving activity carried out in the Spirit – so the apostles' preaching and the deacons' food distribution are both 'ministry'. But, used particularly, 'ministry' refers to special acts of Spirit-inspired service for particular individuals – to personal, private serving rather like a first-century house-servant.

This means that we can use 'ministry' in a general sense to describe all Jesus' life and work, for all his speaking, praying and serving were 'in the Spirit' and characterised by humble service. But we can also use 'ministry' to describe those activities of Jesus which served particular individuals. This is why preaching is ministry only in the *general* sense of the word, not in the narrow and more literal sense; and why, for example, counselling, healing and casting out demons are ministry in both the *general and particular* senses of the word.

This is not a pointless distinction, for a wrong use of words can paralyse the church. Ephesians 4:12 shows that all saints are meant to be equipped by the leaders for the work of ministry. But saints will not minister biblically if they understand ministry only to mean preaching and teaching, or think that they are only called only to practical types of service.

We need to appreciate that, precisely because it is *diakonia*, our ministry should have an essentially personal application, and that we are therefore meant to be led and empowered by the Spirit to serve *particular* individuals. Our serving must be tightly focused.

In the narrow, personal sense of the word, our ministry may involve healing a sick person, or casting out a demon, or counselling, or washing feet, or collecting shopping, or cooking a meal, or praying. But, whatever form it takes, our ministry must be essentially personal and individual, like a house-servant's, and it must always be directed and empowered by the Holy Spirit.

Part Two

Ministers in the Spirit

Once we have grasped that biblical ministry in the Spirit means humble service in the Holy Spirit, we need to establish who ministers in the Spirit in the Scriptures, and what we can learn from their service.

Old Testament ministers

In the Old Testament, a prophet was usually called a 'man of God' – Deuteronomy 33:1; 1 Samuel 2:27; 9:6; 1 Kings 13:1; 20:28; 25:7–9; 2 Kings 4:7; 2 Chronicles 25:7–9 & Nehemiah 12:24. But they were also known as 'servants of God' – the Hebrew word for 'servant', *ebed*, means 'a doer'.

The phrase 'the servant of God' is given only to Moses – Deuteronomy 34:5 & Joshua 8:31. But 'his' 'your' and 'my' servant are used of the other prophets – Jeremiah 44:4; Ezekiel 38:17; Daniel 9:6; Zechariah 1:6. The servant relationship that the prophets enjoyed with God is clearly seen in 2 Kings 17:13 & Ezra 9:11. They were God's mouthpieces and were under orders to pass on his message and not alter it in any way. We can call them God's Old Testament 'ministers'.

Three Hebrew words are used to describe a 'prophet':

- ◆ *Nabi* means one who calls and is called: prophets – servants – ministers – are called *by* God, they call to people *from* God, and they call to God *for* people

- ◆ *Roeh* & *hozeh* are different forms of 'to see': they mean one who sees and is seen; prophets see God, see what God is doing, see events, and are seen by men and women.

These words suggest the basis of ministry in the Spirit. We are called by God to himself, and then call from him to people;

23

we see what God is doing, and are seen by people when we serve as God's 'doers'.

How did they become prophets?
In the Old Testament, prophets had to be chosen by God. All the different accounts of a prophet's calling demonstrate the power of God's call. They had to choose either to set aside what they were doing and begin something which appeared to be difficult, or to disobey God – Exodus 3:1–4:17; Isaiah 6; Jeremiah 1:4–19; Ezekiel 3; Hosea 1:2; Amos 7:14–15 & Jonah 1:1.

The primary object of the call was not to send them on a divine errand, but to summon them into the presence of the holy God. When they had stood before him they could stand before kings and nations. When they had listened to his call, they could call to others. This listening is the heart of all ministry in the Spirit. We see this in 1 Kings 22; Jeremiah 23:22 & Amos 3:7.

What did their ministry involve?
God's servants were involved with three main activities:

1. Speaking God's words
The heart of their message was always 'get right with God'. They pronounced warnings about the future which they validated by examples of God's past dealings; they called the ungodly to repentance by describing the wrath to come; and they offered blessing, calling the godly to holiness – Amos 5; Zephaniah 1:14–2:3; Hosea 5 & Isaiah 2:2–5. They also called God's people to care for the poor and needy – Leviticus 19:9–18; Deuteronomy 23:15–25; 2 Chronicles 28:9–15; Amos 2:6–7; 4:1–3 & 8:4–8.

The prophets reminded people of what God had done; they used the past to proclaim God's nature, and then they revealed what God was about to do. This was not inspired guesswork, but divine revelation. They did not make projections; they prophesied. They spoke to others what they had heard God say to them – Isaiah 41:21–23 & 45:20–22.

2. Pleading with God

God's servants were the only people in the Old Testament who could intercede with God for situations and people. Abraham, the first person directly named as a prophet, is described as being able to plead successfully with God and change a situation – Genesis 20:7.

Jethro suggested that Moses should make intercession his priority, and Moses implemented his advice – Exodus 18:19 & Numbers 27:5. The prophets were known as such powerful intercessors that kings begged them to plead with God on their behalf – 1 Kings 13:6; 2 Kings 19:4 & Zechariah 7:1–3.

3. Doing God's deeds

God's servants were the only people in the Old Testament who were involved with the miraculous – with signs and wonders, healing, counselling, and speaking with God's prophetic authority.

Only those men and women who had been anointed with God's Spirit were able to be 'doers' of God's deeds – Genesis 20; Numbers 12; 1 Kings 13; 17:7–24; 2 Kings 4:8–37; 20:1–11; 2 Chronicles 25:5–16 & Jeremiah 38:14–28. We return to this later.

How were they inspired to minister?

1. The Word of God

Amos 3:8 shows that the Word of God had a dynamic impact upon the prophets. 'The Word of the Lord came to' is the most frequent phrase which describes this type of inspiration. 'Came to' is better rendered as either 'became actively present to' or, more simply, 'was to'. This expression describes an internal awareness of God's message which grows over a period of time – for example, Zechariah 1:1 & 7.

As we see in Jeremiah 1:11; 18:1–4; 24 & Amos 7:7, this prompting sometimes stemmed from ordinary events. It seems that God unveiled his word in the intimacy of private fellowship with his servant, rather than with a sudden flash of illumination. This is inspiration as the result of meditation, reflection, observation and study.

2. The burden of God

Habakkuk 1:1 describes the *massa* of the Lord. Some translations render this as 'message' or 'oracle', but literally it is a 'load' or 'burden'. It carries the picture of God allowing his servant to feel what he feels – Isaiah 13:1; 14:28; 15:1; 17:1; 19:1; 21:1, 11, 13; 22:1; 23:1 & Jeremiah 23:33–40.

3. The Spirit of God

Scripture teaches such a strong association between the Spirit and prophecy that it almost cannot be overstated.

Numbers 11:29 is the first link; 1 Samuel 10 & 1 Samuel 19:18–24 show that the descent of the Spirit led to spontaneous prophecy. Micah 3:8 suggests that the Spirit was not only the source of inspiration for God's servants but also that he gave them the necessary courage to deliver the revelation. And Joel 2:28 makes it clear that receiving the Spirit should result in the activity of divine prophesying – of speaking God's words, to particular people, in God's power. This is instant inspiration for immediate delivery.

4. Dreams, visions and angels

God's servants laid claim to frequent inspiration through visions by day and dreams by night – Numbers 12:6; Isaiah 6; Ezekiel 40:2; Daniel 7:1 & Zechariah 1:8. On rare occasions, angels were sent to prophets – 2 Kings 1:3–15; 1 Chronicles 21:18; Daniel 9:21 & Zechariah 1:9.

We examine the way that the prophets were inspired by God in much more detail in the *Sword of the Spirit* volume *Listening to God*.

How did they minister?

Although all the Old Testament prophets were inspired by the same God, they each had a distinctive style of speech and ministry.

Prophets merely passed on the revelation that they had received from God. Revelation, however, is not dictation; so the prophets stamped their own personalities on the revelations and spoke them in a variety of styles. Narrative verse, prose, parables, direct speech, satire, psalms, laments, sermons, diatribe, *midrash* – all these, and more methods of proclaiming, were used by God's servants to pass on God's revelation.

When God's servants spoke in the Spirit, they did not express an opinion – they brought an authoritative utterance which altered the situation. What they announced happened. Isaiah 40:6–8 and Isaiah 55:11 reveal the awesome power of the prophetic spoken word.

Some prophets used symbolic, dramatic acts as part of their prophesying. These were not visual aids, but prophetic deeds which proclaimed what God had said and thought – for example, Exodus 17:9; Jeremiah 19:1, 10–11 & Ezekiel 4:1–3.

Other prophets used miracles. In fact, the only Old Testament miracle workers were prophets: Moses, Elijah and Elisha are obvious examples, but we also see this in 1 Kings 13:1–10.

Every aspect of Old Testament prophetic ministry is extremely relevant to our ministry in the Spirit today. All the principles of careful listening to God, being inspired by the Word and the Spirit, and speaking out God's words with God's authority are the essential biblical foundation to all ministry in the Spirit.

Jesus the minister

Deuteronomy 18:15–20 prepares Israel for the leadership of Joshua, but also prophesies that God will send another healing, miracle-working, law-giving prophet like Moses.

At the time of Christ, the Jews expected the coming Messiah to be this 'another Moses' – a prophet to whom God would reveal himself as he had in Numbers 12:6–8; and who would repeat, on a grand scale, the exploits of the Exodus.

When the priests and Levites questioned John the Baptist, in John 1:19–25, they wanted to establish if he was 'the Prophet'. And Acts 3:22–24 shows that Peter believed Christ to be this Prophet.

Time and again, Jesus was recognised by the people as a prophet – Matthew 21:11; Luke 24:19; John 4:18; 6:14 & 7:52. In Matthew 13:57 Jesus seemed to consider himself to be a prophet. Certainly, he manifested all the signs of an extraordinary prophet right through his ministry and followed all their principles of ministry in the Spirit.

- ◆ Prophets are close to the Father's heart – John 1:18 shows that Jesus is nearest of all to the Father's heart.

- ◆ Prophets share God's secrets – Matthew 11:27 suggests a degree of intimacy unparalleled even by Moses.

- ◆ Prophets are God's servants – the Gospel of John reveals Jesus as one totally under his Father's authority. It shows that he never goes anywhere, does anything, or acts, except in obedient response to an initiative from the Spirit.

- ◆ Prophets are given a specific commission – Matthew 15:24 shows that Jesus was sent to a defined area with a unique calling.

- ◆ Prophets are God's mouthpiece – John 12:49–50 reports that Jesus claimed no originality for his speech. Everything he spoke was what the Father had told him to say.

- ◆ Only prophets used to heal the sick – the John 9 beggar identified Jesus as a prophet because his eyes had been opened.

- ◆ Only prophets intercede with God – Romans 8:34 reveals Jesus as the Intercessor.

- ◆ Only prophets pass on God's counsel to people – Isaiah 9:6 points to Jesus as the wonder-counsellor.

- ◆ Prophets are anointed with the Spirit – John 3:34 shows that Jesus was anointed without measure.

The Old Testament identification of the Spirit with prophecy is brought to a climax in Jesus. In Acts 10:38, Peter quoted

Isaiah 61:1 and applied it to Jesus. His baptism was the pivotal point of Jesus' life. As he rose from the river, the Spirit came down. In that moment Jesus was revealed as the *Christos* – the anointed. He was set apart as a beloved Spirit-anointed prophet to serve and to minister in the Spirit.

In Matthew 3:1–12; Mark 1:1–8; Luke 3:1–18 & John 1:19–34, John the Baptist introduced Jesus as the one who would baptise in the Holy Spirit. Jesus' first prophetic, ascended activity was to anoint his Church with the Holy Spirit – to set the Church apart as a race of prophets. His second prophetic act – and this will continue until he comes – was, and is, to intercede at the Father's right hand for us.

Yet Jesus was much more than just another prophet. Acts 10:43 shows that his birth, life, ministry, death, resurrection, ascension and Pentecostal activity confirmed all that the Old Testament prophets had foretold – over 300 detailed prophecies were fulfilled in his life.

Revelation 19:10 instructs that all prophecy should be operated by the Spirit of Jesus *and* must bear testimony to him. This means that Jesus is the supreme prophet, and that all who prophesy must point to him. He is both our example in ministry *and* the object of our ministry.

We are called to *serve like Jesus* by ministering only in the power of the Spirit; but we must also remember that we *serve Jesus* by our ministering in the Spirit. This means that, when we reach out to needy people because the Spirit has prompted us, Jesus is ministering with us through the Spirit, *and* that Jesus is the one to whom we are ultimately ministering.

New Testament ministers

The New Testament introduced a new age and a new organisation for prophetic ministry. It retained the basic Old Testament understanding, but the Church, rather than isolated individuals, became the centre of prophetic ministry. This means that prophetic ministry should be at the centre of every expression of the Church today.

In Numbers 11:16–17 & 24–30, Moses needed help, but his prophetic burden could be shared only with those on whom the Spirit came. When Joshua queried Eldad and Medad's prophesying, Moses responded with a prophetic prayer which has rung through the ages: 'Oh that all the Lord's people were prophets, and that the Lord would put his Spirit upon them!'

God heard and honoured this prayer at Pentecost – when he poured out his Spirit without restriction upon the Church. Since Pentecost, the possibility of prophetic ministry in the Spirit has been open to every believer in the Church who has been filled with the Holy Spirit.

At Pentecost, there was no limitation on the giving of the Spirit and no restriction on the receiving. And when Peter spoke about prophecy, in Acts 2:18, he surely understood his words to mean that the whole Church would perpetuate and expand the ministry of the Old Testament prophets. This means that all people in the Church – men and women, old and young, educated and illiterate – can minister in the Spirit.

Since Pentecost, the whole people of God can be genuine, anointed servants of God. All believers can be 'called and calling', 'seen and seeing'; all can enter into the presence of the Holy God and hear his secrets; all can pass on God's thoughts and speak with God's authority and effectiveness; all can intercede for others and be inspired by the Word and the 'Spirit'; all can pass on God's counsel and healing. Every believer can now minister in the Spirit like the prophets of old.

The Acts 2:18 promise is not that all will be prophets, but that all shall prophesy. This is an important distinction. The prophesying of the New Testament church is seen in the everyday behaviour of the saints in the book of Acts – in their Spirit-directed serving. But there still remained those who were called 'prophets'.

It is the same in some other areas of ministry. All believers are commissioned to evangelise, but not all are evangelists; all are commanded to heal; but not all are healers; all are called to teach, but not all are teachers. We may not all be employed by a church as a fully-paid minister, but we are all called to be involved full-time in prophetic activity – by listening to God, speaking his words and doing his deeds.

Ministry in the market place

This helps us understand the true ministry of the Church. We are called to minister like Jesus did. This means we represent him, doing his works not just in the meeting place (the church) but also the market place (the world). During the height of the Charismatic movement, during the 1970s and 1980s, preachers and teachers placed much emphasis on the 'gifts of the Spirit'. Their goal was to see the body of Christ equipped with the prophetic and charismatic enablements of the Spirit so that every member could function as God intended for the up-building of the Church according to Ephesians 4:12–16. This contrasted with the strong emphasis among other evangelical pastors which focused on practical areas of service within the church – such as, stewarding, serving food, cleaning, and polishing brass. We have seen that all service is ministry in the general sense, and that both the exercise of spiritual gifts and practical works of service, are truly ministry.

But the need now is for a greater understanding of the ministry itself, that is, the ministry of Christ to which every member of the body is called. The ministry of Christ is simply the work of Christ that he calls us to do as his body, his agent on the earth. In John 20:21, Jesus said to his disciples, 'As the Father has sent me, I also send you'. Jesus' 'sending' mission of the Church is also seen in Matthew 9:38; Matthew 10:16; Mark 3:14 & 6:7.

We can easily see that the ministry of Christ has to do with the Church. We are called to minister to one another, and to build one another up. But the sending of Jesus is far wider than that. In fact, the main thrust of Jesus' sending has to do with the world. We are sent by Christ into the world in order to minister for him and to do his work.

This has enormous implications for those who are concerned about 'ministry in the Spirit'. It is not just about learning how to serve one another through the gifts of the Spirit or to serve in the church through practical matters such as flower rotas or coffee duties. The ministry is doing what Jesus did – the full range of his ministry to others. And, most important of all, doing this in the market place – not just the meeting place. In other words, Christ's goal in ministry is not just to see more people doing work in the church, either through spiritual gifts or practical service, but to mobilise the whole church to work in the world.

Jesus' Great Commission to the Church in Matthew 28:18–20 is to make disciples, showing that our being sent has to do with going with his mandate into the *market place*, ministering as he did, and serving in the power of the Spirit. Our service will not necessarily be through holding official 'ministry positions' in the church, but has to do with serving Christ and others in the world wherever he sends us. True ministers of Christ are the members of his body who evangelise, teach, heal, deliver and disciple others, serving Christ in these ways as students in college, business people, politicians, doctors, teachers, workers in factories, offices, or farms – indeed wherever we are in our daily life.

As you read on and learn how to minister like Jesus did, to minister in the Spirit, bear in mind that you have already been called to do the work of Jesus, right where you are. Bear in mind that God has given you a ready made sphere of service, in your home, your family and in your daily place of occupation.

Part Three

Ministering in the Spirit

We have seen that the ministry we are called to is 'in the Spirit'. We are called to serve God and each other with the care and humility of a first century domestic servant *and* with the power, anointing and authority of an Old Testament prophet.

The anointing of the Spirit at Pentecost did not clothe the Church with some sort of magical power for ministry, instead it introduced the Church into a living relationship with the Holy Spirit. The disciples were plunged into the Spirit so that they could be in him and with him for ever, so that they could live and serve in permanent partnership with the Spirit. The promised 'Helper' of John 14:16 had come alongside to dwell with the Church and help them to witness effectively to Jesus.

It is the same for us. When we claim by faith the promised anointing of the Spirit, we are anointed with him, we are dipped into him, and we are filled with him. We start to walk in and with him, and we can minister at his prompting, using his gifts, with his power and effectiveness. We examine this in *Knowing the Spirit*.

Developing the ministry of Jesus

We have seen that every aspect of prophetic activity and ministry is meant to point to Jesus, and we know that Spirit's only purpose is to glorify Jesus. This means that we minister in the Spirit so that Jesus' ministry can continue and he can be glorified.

Discipleship

Ministry in the Spirit is always in the context of discipleship – both ministering as an expression of our own discipleship and making disciples through our ministry to others. Jesus' first partners in ministry were the 'disciples' and his ministry commission to them was to make disciples of others. The Greek word *mathetes* means 'learner'. Like Jesus' first disciples, we need 'to learn' from Christ and follow his example in everything – in our thinking, speaking, living, praying, compassion, serving, ministry and morality.

Discipleship means obeying Jesus completely because we love him and want to learn only from him, and it also means teaching others to do the same. When we live in the Spirit, we are bound to hear the Spirit prompting us to think and act like Jesus. We will 'feel' his prompting to do this, go there, sit quietly, speak a brief sentence, and so on. But remember, the Spirit never forces us to obey him, and he never deserts us – not even when we make mistakes or act foolishly. He is always 'called alongside us'.

Guidance
All ministry depends on our ability to listen to the Spirit and to test and recognise his prompting. This was the key secret of Jesus' effectiveness. If we are to develop Jesus' ministry, we simply have to learn how to tell the difference between the Spirit's prompting, our natural thoughts, and devilish confusion. We examine this in *Listening to God*.

We can be sure that, if we are living in the Spirit, he will guide and direct us. But he does not compel us to obey him. He encourages. He advises. He persists. But he never insists.

Many believers pray only to the Father, but it is sometimes helpful to pray in a more conversational way with the Spirit. Of course, we intercede *with* the Spirit, not *to* the Spirit, but we can *talk* with the Spirit in fellowship and in dependence on his help. If we are serious about ministering in and with the Holy Spirit, it should be clear that we really will need to listen to him.

Depending on the Spirit
We start to make spiritual progress only when we grasp that we really can do absolutely nothing on our own. It is only by depending completely on the Spirit that we can minister in the Spirit.

I Kings 18 illustrates the differences between a Spirit-filled prophet and false-prophets. The important point for us here is that Elijah did not try to make anything happen, instead he did everything possible to prove to the people that *he* was not responsible for the miracle. Like Elijah, we need to make it difficult for people to think that what happens in ministry is due to human manipulation or pressure. We need to make it as clear as possible that it is the Spirit or nothing.

This principle is very clear in Jesus' ministry, for example, John 5:30. Time and again, Jesus insisted that he could do nothing, say nothing and go nowhere on his own authority: it was God or nothing.

A striking feature of Jesus' ministry is the way that he sometimes asked people to tell nobody about the miracle. Mark 7:31–37 & 8:22–26 illustrate his holy desire to work unobtrusively – which is one of the hallmarks of the humble, self-effacing Spirit.

When we genuinely and fully depend on the Spirit of truth, we will surely be characterised by his straightforward speech, and will not feel the need to use worldly methods which overstate facts, ignore mistakes, and rarely focus all attention on Jesus.

The Spirit's anointing

Depending on the Spirit means relying on our anointing with him. There is a terrible temptation in ministry to rely more on our personal experience, and the experience of others, than on the prompting and guidance of the Spirit. But we must never forget the anointing of the Holy Spirit and we will do well to remember that the whole of Jesus' ministry was conducted under the anointing of the Spirit. As we see in *Knowing the Spirit*, it was only after his anointing with the Spirit that Jesus began his public ministry. Jesus chose not to use his divine nature when ministering because he was modelling the way for us to minister and therefore relied just as much on prayer, the Word, the anointing and the gifts of the Spirit as we do. If Jesus needed the anointing of the Spirit for his ministry on earth, how much more must we need the same anointing to do everything that God has called us to do?

Of course, we must always follow biblical principles, and both common sense and experience are important, but we must depend consciously on the Spirit and submit to his authority at all times.

Discerning the Spirit's agenda

It is a basic principle of ministry that God does not give power for what he is not doing, but that he always provides power for what he is doing. This is why the Old Testament prophets were called God's *ebed*, 'doers' or servants.

Jesus, who was fully God and – as a man – had been anointed with the Spirit without measure, did not heal all who were sick in the nation! Instead, he healed all who were brought to him and also took God's healing to specific individuals. But he often ignored crowds of sick people around the one he was healing. Clearly, Jesus did only what the Father was doing and stuck rigidly to the Spirit's agenda.

Our ministry will be ineffective if we try to take the initiative or follow our own inclination. We must wait for the Holy Spirit and receive specific directions and revelation from him before we proceed in any form of active ministry in the Spirit. This is exactly what we see in the Old Testament prophets.

Waiting

Knowing God's will is one of the hardest parts of the Christian life. We long to obey God, but we do not always know what he wants us to do. Instead of waiting for direction, many believers often presume and do whatever seems to be best according to their own thinking or inclination at that moment.

John 10:16 & 27 are promises which Jesus has kept. By the Spirit, we do hear God's voice. Sometimes, however, we are not sure whether it is his voice or our own thoughts. At other times, our minds are so full of clutter that we cannot hear his voice clearly. We know that he is speaking to us, but we cannot make out what he is saying.

We need to wait patiently on God – creating a place of peace in our lives, perhaps through meditating on his Word – before we start listening for the Spirit's direction.

Listening

We need to spend more time listening in prayer than we do. Too often, we spend time asking God to do things rather than asking him what he wants us to do – and listening for his reply.

We must recognise that God usually speaks to us, as to the prophets of old, through his Word – so we must spend time listening to God by reading the Scriptures. But we need to be continuously alert because God sometimes speaks his word to us through ordinary events. And we must watch out for any prophetic 'burden' of the Lord which develops in us and is God's way of directing our attention to his concerns.

At a practical level, asking God specific questions is a good way of learning to identify God's voice. We should not be frightened to ask him what we should do or say. But we must 'test' the thoughts which come into our mind.

The gift of 'discerning of spirits', referred to in 1 Corinthians 12:10, is given, in part, to help us determine God's word. The Greek word *diakrisis* is often translated as 'discerning', but it literally means 'separating'. The gift of *diakrisis* refers to the Spirit-given insight which enables us to 'separate' the divine from the demonic or the human.

When listening to God, we often 'hear' or 'see' a message or instruction which is a mixture of God's divine direction and our human enthusiasm and cultural values. The gift of *diakrisis*, 'discerning' or 'separating', of spirits helps us to 'sieve out' the human elements and establish the core divine word from God. We examine this more fully in *Listening to God*.

Once we have identified God's word we must act on what we have understood in our inner spirits. With time and a serious commitment to being a 'learner', we do begin to recognise the Spirit's special way of speaking to us.

We should never stop spending time alone with the Spirit listening to him, but we will also increasingly recognise his way of interrupting our natural thoughts when he wants us to minister to someone.

We should remember that the prophets were inspired by the Spirit as well as by the Word, and this was instant inspiration for immediate action. Some of the most precious times of ministry occur when we trust these sudden thoughts.

Asking

When we are ministering to a person, we need to listen both to God and to the individual person we are helping.

Jesus did not only function supernaturally, he also worked at the natural level of observation and deduction. He asked normal and natural questions which helped in ministry. If he needed to ask questions like those in Mark 5:9; 8:23; 9:21; Luke 18:41 & John 5:6, so will we.

As well as asking the person questions, we should always ask God what else needs to be known. This means asking God to show us what is happening, what caused the problem, what he wants us to do, and so on. The Spirit may give us a picture or word to pass on, suggest a statement we should make, or put a question into our mind.

Once we have asked all the relevant questions and discerned the Spirit's agenda, we turn to the Holy Spirit for ministry direction.

Demonstrations of the Spirit

When the Spirit prompts us to speak and act, we must remember that we are simply passing on God's words and doing his deeds. We are called to speak with his authority, but we do not heal the sick or cast out demons. We minister in partnership with the Spirit: God is responsible for the miracles, we merely supply the faith, the hands and the mouth.

Faith
Some believers think that they need huge amounts of faith for ministry, whereas Jesus suggested that we need only a tiny amount. Faith is like the clutch in a car. There might be a powerful engine roaring under the bonnet, but the car remains stationery until the driver presses the clutch and slips the gear. The clutch, however, does not make the car move; it merely engages the power.

Matthew 9:2, 22, 29 & Mark 6:1–6 show that sometimes the person being ministered to had faith. This means that when we minister we should be ready to encourage people to believe in God's power and in his promises. It also means we should be firmly persuaded that God can do what is needed, and that we are committed to speaking his words when he prompts us. We examine this more in *Living Faith*.

Gifts
Ministry in the Spirit normally means ministering the gifts of the Spirit. In fact, it is difficult to envisage any form of ministry which does not involve the gifts described in 1 Corinthians 12.

In *Knowing the Spirit*, we see that God's giving of grace-gifts to each believer is a continuous activity and not a once-for-all action. This means that we do not receive spiritual gifts as personal possessions; rather, the Spirit gives us whatever gift we need whenever we need it.

Jesus had tremendous skill in ministering according to the gifts of the Spirit. In fact, we see examples of all the New Testament gifts in Jesus' ministry except tongues and interpretation.

For example, we see Jesus using:

- The gift of faith – Mark 11:20–25 & John 11:41–42
- The gift of miracles – Mark 6:30–52 & John 2:1–11
- The gift of healing – Matthew 4:23–25 & Mark 5:21–43
- The word of wisdom – Matthew 22:18; Luke 13:10–17 & John 7:53–8:4

- ◆ The discerning of spirits – Matthew 16:17–23 & Luke 13:10–17
- ◆ The gift of prophecy – John 2:19
- ◆ The word of knowledge – John 1:47–50 & John 4:16–20.

If Jesus needed the gifts to help him to minister, we can surely expect the same for ourselves. We must, therefore, make sure that we develop expertise and experience in using them effectively.

At its simplest, using the gifts of the Spirit means relying on whatever thoughts or words the Spirit gives us, for the gifts are merely manifestations of the Spirit himself. Isaiah 11:1–2 lists some of the Spirit's attributes which are similar to the gifts; and 11:3–5 shows them being used in godly activity and prophetic authority.

Through the 1 Corinthians 12 gifts, the Spirit reveals some facet of his divine knowledge, ability and nature, and he applies that directly to the situation or person we are serving. 1 Corinthians 12:8–10 identifies nine gifts:

- ◆ The word of wisdom – the Spirit's ability to apply a revelation, or to understand how to resolve or assist a situation
- ◆ The word of knowledge – the Spirit's revelation of facts about a person or situation
- ◆ Healings – the Spirit's insight into how to minister God's healing to a particular person, and his enabling effectively to minister God's healing to the person
- ◆ Faith – a supernatural surge of the Spirit's confidence in God's ability to do something seemingly impossible
- ◆ Miracles – the Spirit's miraculous power intervening in the natural order through a minister
- ◆ Prophecy – the Spirit's message for a person, group of people or situation

◆ Discerning of spirits – the Spirit's insight which identifies the motivating spirit behind a word or person, and helps us to separate the divine from the human and the demonic

◆ Different kinds of tongues – the Spirit's words to pray in an unlearnt language

◆ Interpretation of tongues – the Spirit's revelation of the gist of a prayer in tongues.

It should be plain that these gifts are important tools which really do help us enormously in ministry. Obviously we will make mistakes when we start to use them. But we will develop more skill in manifesting the gifts if we persevere through the failures and errors.

Ministry

When we are ministering, the Spirit guides us along his own creative path. He might prompt us to do something unusual – like Jesus anointing a man's eyes with saliva. But this does not mean that we should repeat what has 'worked' in the past, or ever do the same thing again, unless he clearly instructs us to do so.

In later chapters, we consider some practical suggestions for different elements of ministry, but the basic principle always remains the same – we listen to the Spirit, we test his words, we depend on him and his gifts, and we do only what he prompts us to do.

Discipleship with the Spirit

In Luke 17:15–19; John 5:14 & 9:35–38 we see that Jesus followed through *after* ministry with many of the people he served. He was careful to make disciples and not just 'meet the needs' of the people he served.

People do not always receive everything from God when we minister to them for the first time. We often need to go back to them many times to help them receive whatever God has for them. As we will see in Part Eleven, this is especially true in the ministry of counselling, where our ministry to a specific person may continue for some time.

We must recognise that we have a special God-given responsibility for the people we serve. It is rarely adequate to lay hands on someone, pray a quick prayer, and then pass on to the next person. True 'ministry in the Spirit' always communicates the Spirit's 'called alongside' commitment to people, and we must never avoid expressing this.

Obviously, we should always pray for the safety and spiritual development of each person we serve, but we need the Spirit's guidance as to how closely we should be involved with each individual.

We know that the Spirit has come alongside to encourage, teach, comfort, and direct us. When we are ministering in him, we will naturally be led alongside people to serve and encourage them in a similarly committed and positive way.

Corporate ministry
The principle of partnership in ministry runs through the Bible. For example, Jesus ministered with the apostles; he sent them to minister in pairs; he sent the seventy disciples to minister in pairs; there was a team of seven Spirit-filled 'deacons'; Paul always ministered with a close companion and a small team; and a group of elders was appointed in every New Testament church. We consider this in Parts Seven & Eight of *Glory in the Church*. Ministry in the Spirit should be the natural development of your own discipleship, which, as we emphasise in Part Eleven of *Glory in the Church*, is best done within the context of small groups or cells. Your cell leaders will be able to model to you how to minister in the Spirit and help you begin to step out also. But all ministry should be conducted in partnership with others who are in good fellowship with the church, not as an independent activity.

This does not mean that we always refuse to minister if nobody is with us. Acts contains many examples of believers who were sent by the Spirit to minister on their own – for example, Acts 8:26–40 & 9:10–19.

When we minister in partnership, it is easier to lead the people we serve into similar human relationships within the body of Christ. Our ministry in the Spirit must encourage people into a corporate life which reflects the eternal relationships which exist within the Godhead, and which strengthen and build the Church in its inherent, cross-forged oneness.

Part Four

The basis of healing ministry

One of the most obvious ways Jesus serves individual people in the New Testament is by healing them. But before we examine the way that he ministers through healing, we need to appreciate that his healing ministry is firmly based in the Old Testament. We usually think of healing ministry in connection with the New Testament only, but the Old Testament provides us with an understanding that healing is part of God's nature and intention. In Luke 4:16–20, for example, Jesus introduces himself to Israel as the one who has been sent to heal by stating that he is the fulfilment of Isaiah 61:1–2.

This introduction to the Son is rather like Exodus 15:26, where the Father identifies himself to the people of Israel as *Yahweh Rapha*, 'the Lord who heals you'. Throughout the Scriptures, the entire ministry of the Father and Son is based upon these parallel divine revelations that healing is central to the nature and ministry of God.

The Old Testament presents God as being concerned with the hygiene and nutrition of his people, as binding up their broken-hearts, as comforting and counselling them, and as healing them of diseases. We see this in, for example, Exodus 15:26; Leviticus 7:22–27; 11:1–15:33; 17:1–16; Psalm 34:18; 86:17 & Isaiah 61:1–2. This means that Jesus' healing ministry is not something new; rather it is a development of God's healing work in the Old Testament.

Healing in the Old Testament

The Old Testament includes more material about the healing ministry of God than is often supposed. It contains a range of promises.

Promises of health and healing
The Old Testament promises:

◆ Health as a blessing following from personal or national obedience

◆ Healing through the natural processes which God built into humanity through creation

◆ Supernatural sovereign healing intervention

◆ Supernatural healing intervention in response to repentance

◆ Supernatural healing intervention in response to intercession.

We see these promises in passages like Exodus 15:26; Deuteronomy 5:33; 7:15; 32:39; 2 Chronicles 30:20; Psalm 23:1–2; 34:19–20; 38:3–10; 41:3; 69:29–30; 91:10–16; 103:1–4; 107:20; 116:8; 145:14; 146:8; 147:3; Proverbs 3:7–10; 4:20–23; 9:11; 16:24; 17:22; Ecclesiastes 3:3; Isaiah 19:22; 30:26; 32:3; 35:5; 40:27–31; 41:10; 53:4–6; 57:18–19; 58:8; Jeremiah 17:14; 30:17; Ezekiel 16:6; 47:1–12; Hosea 6:1; 13:14 & Malachi 4:2.

It is evident from this list that there are multiple references to healing in each of the major Jewish divisions of the Old Testament – the Law, the Prophets and the Writings. This illustrates the importance of God's role as healer in the Old Testament.

Promises of fertility
Exodus 23:25–26 & Deuteronomy 7:12–15 are important healing passages, and both promise fertility as a special blessing for obedience. We examine this aspect of blessing later, but we should recognise now the scriptural importance of fertility.

We see this in, for example, Genesis 1:28; 9:1; 12:2; 17:16–20; 22:17; 24:35–36; 26:3–4, 24; 28:3; 30:30; 32:12; 35:11; 46:3; 48:3, 15–16; Deuteronomy 7:12–14; Job 5:25; Psalm 127:3–5 & 128:3–4.

Promises of long life
Although a long life is a natural consequence of health and healing, the Old Testament emphasises that, in Israel, national and personal longevity are linked – like fertility – to obedience.

This promise can be seen, for example, in Exodus 20:12; 23:25–26; Leviticus 18:5; Deuteronomy 5:33; 6:2–3; 30:15–19 & Job 5:26.

Prayers and testimonies of healing
The Old Testament also records many examples of people claiming these promises in prayer and many testimonies of answered prayer: for example, Genesis 25:21; 30:6, 17, 22–23; Exodus 1:7, 9, 20; Deuteronomy 1:10–11; 1 Samuel 1:10–2:11; 1 Kings 4:20; Psalm 6:2; 30:2; 41:4; 107:20; 147:3 & Jeremiah 17:14.

Examples of healing

The Old Testament also describes nine incidents of healing. These illustrate the biblical basis for the healing ministry which is fulfilled and developed by Jesus in his ministry, and is relevant for us today.

Genesis 20:1–18
The cure of Abimelech is the first scriptural example of healing ministry, and it lays down several important principles.

Abraham, the minister, is a prophet. This begins the link between prophetic activity and healing which runs through the Bible.

God answered Abraham's prayers and used him in healing ministry even though he had been sinfully deceiving Abimelech.

Abimelech was a pagan king. This suggests that healing ministry includes the interaction between God's servants and people who do not serve and follow God.

God sent the sickness as some sort of curse or punishment, but – through prophetic intercession – God revoked his action. For Abimelech, the healing was a sign pointing to forgiveness.

Several months must have passed before Abimelech had convincing proof of the cure. The miracle may have been instant, but Abimelech's appreciation of the healing must have been gradual.

Abraham's faith is a vital part of the ministry.

Numbers 12:1–16

Miriam's healing from leprosy underlines many of these ideas. Moses, a prophet, ministered the healing; Miriam's sickness was sent by God as a punishment; the healing pointed to her forgiveness; and the miracle was not revealed instantly to anybody.

Unlike Abimelech, Miriam was one of God's servants, and she was also given an action to perform which facilitated her healing.

1 Kings 13:1–24

This story shows that there can be a place for fasting in healing, and that God's servants must always obey God's orders unconditionally.

The death of the prophet shows how seriously God takes his instructions; we must never think that we can treat the Spirit's promptings lightly.

1 Kings 17:8–24

A widow's son died and she blamed Elijah. The prophet took the boy's body, carried it to his bed, then cried out to God in intercession.

Elijah did not have a precedent for his prayers, but that did not stop him praying. None of us would ever minister if we restricted our serving to those things we had already seen God perform through us!

2 Kings 4:8–37

2 Kings 2:9–15 reports that Elisha inherited a double portion of Elijah's prophetic anointing. It is instructive, therefore, to note that more Old Testament healing ministry is associated with Elisha than with anyone else – and that most of the people served by Elisha were pagans. This underlines the link between the Spirit's anointing, ministry and mission.

2 Kings 4:8–37 relates two episodes. A woman was very hospitable, and this prompted Elisha to offer to speak to the king on her behalf. When she made it clear that she did not want a material reward, Elisha announced that she would give birth to a son in twelve months' time.

Again, there must have been a delayed appreciation of the healing. The woman would not have had evidence of conception for many months, or of the child's sex until it was born. In the Scriptures, there is usually a gap between God's word and convincing proof that it has come to pass – and God often calls us also to live with similar faith in the gap between his word and our experience.

The woman gave birth to a boy who later died. But her faith in Elisha remained absolute – he had obtained a son for her, therefore he could restore him. Elisha gave Gehazi his staff, a symbol of his prophetic authority, and sent him to stretch it over the corpse. When nothing happened, the prophet came himself and prayed personally.

2 Kings 5:1–27

Elisha sent his servant Gehazi with the details of a task which Naaman had to fulfil to facilitate the healing. Naaman's indignation, in verse 11, shows he needed to learn that healing ministry is a matter of obedience, not technique, and that it is always due to divine intervention and never to human exertion.

After the healing, Naaman recognised that Yahweh alone was truly God and pressed Elisha to accept a gift. Elisha refused. He knew that human ministers should take no credit or reward for something that God alone has done. Instead of thanking man, Naaman praised God. He rode off, healed and blessed, the first scriptural example of a convert through the healing ministry.

In Luke 4:27, Jesus looked back to this story and claimed it as the precedent for his entire ministry. This illustrates just how important it is to understand the Old Testament before studying Jesus' ministry.

2 Kings 13:20–21
There appears to be no faith exercised and no prayer offered in this incident – only fear and panic. All we can say for certain is that it shows God is not tame or predictable. He cannot be imprisoned in techniques and traditions of ministry. He works how, when, and through whom he wills.

2 Kings 20:1–11
The prophet Isaiah was sent by God to announce the king's imminent death. Hezekiah pleaded with God, and God heard his prayer. So Isaiah was sent back to announce three things, including a healing.

In this story, God's minister is given a task to carry out – only then does the king recover. Again, it is unlikely that there was immediate evidence of the cure, for the king asked for proof that he would survive the next three days – which God graciously supplied through his anointed servant.

Basic principles

Although these Old Testament stories mainly emphasise the sovereignty and power of God, ten basic principles of biblical healing ministry begin to emerge.

- ◆ The healing ministry was exclusive to God's servants the prophets – God worked in partnership *only* with and through those whom he had anointed with his Spirit as prophets.
- ◆ The sickness healed was occasionally due to personal sin.
- ◆ In some cases, either the minister or the sick person needed to perform an action as part of the healing ministry.
- ◆ The prophetic minister either interceded with God for the healing or announced its arrival – which could be as far as a year away.

◆ The prophets did not go about offering healing ministry indiscriminately. Instead they responded to human requests and to God's prompting through the Spirit.

◆ The people they ministered to were not necessarily Jews – more than half were pagans outside the covenant.

◆ Some element of faith or expectancy was normally present.

◆ Many of the healings would not have appeared to be instant – there was often a delay before it was obvious that healing had taken place.

◆ Many of the healings were signs directing the sick person's attention to something more significant – often to forgiveness.

◆ Sometimes none of these principles applied, and God intervened in a sovereign and mysterious way.

Part Five

Healing in the New Testament

Jesus always was the Son of God, but few people suspected his divinity or prophetic office until after his anointing with the Spirit at his baptism. This was the moment when the Father publicly anointed Jesus with the Spirit to commission and equip him for his messianic task.

In Luke's account, Jesus left the river filled with the Spirit; he was driven into the desert by the Spirit; he overcame satanic temptation; and then – full of the power of the Spirit – he returned to his home synagogue to introduce himself as the fulfilment of Isaiah 61:1–2. Luke 4:23 makes it clear that Jesus had already begun his healing ministry by the time he returned to Nazareth, but links Jesus' announcement in Nazareth to his anointing in the river.

Luke 4:16–30 describes Jesus proclaiming that, because he had been anointed with the Spirit, he was now healing the broken-hearted, liberating the oppressed and giving new sight to the blind. Here, Jesus is describing the basic elements of genuine 'ministry in the Spirit'.

In the synagogue, Jesus identified himself as a prophet and linked himself with the Old Testament prophets' healing ministries. He was claiming to be another healing prophet whose ministry, like Elijah and Elisha's, was mainly to those who are outside God's kingdom.

Jesus' healing ministry

The Gospels accredit about twenty specific healing incidents to Jesus. (This does not include the occasions when he set people free from evil spirits – we will study these later.):

- ◆ The nobleman's son at Capernaum – John 4:43–54

- ◆ Jairus' daughter – Matthew 9:18–26; Mark 5:21–43 & Luke 8:40–56
- ◆ The woman with the issue of blood – Matthew 9:20–22; Mark 5:25–34 & Luke 8:43–48
- ◆ Two blind men – Matthew 9:27–31
- ◆ The paralysed man let down through the roof – Matthew 9:1–8; Mark 2:2–12 & Luke 5:17–26
- ◆ A leper – Matthew 8:1–4; Mark 1:40–45 & Luke 5:12–14
- ◆ The centurion's servant – Matthew 8:5–13 & Luke 7:1–10
- ◆ Peter's mother-in-law – Matthew 8:14–15; Mark 1:29–31 & Luke 4:38–39
- ◆ The widow of Nain's son – Luke 7:11–17
- ◆ The lame man at the pool of Bethesda – John 5:1–18
- ◆ The man born blind – John 9:1–41
- ◆ The man with the withered hand – Matthew 12:9–14; Mark 3:1–6 & Luke 6:6–11
- ◆ The woman bent double – Luke 13:10–17
- ◆ The man with dropsy – Luke 14:1–6
- ◆ The ten lepers – Luke 17:11–19
- ◆ The deaf and dumb man – Mark 7:31–37
- ◆ The blind man of Bethsaida – Mark 8:22–26
- ◆ Lazarus – John 11:1–44
- ◆ The blind men of Jericho – Matthew 20:29–34 & Luke 18:35–43
- ◆ The high priest's servant – Luke 22:47–51.

The Gospels also record twelve general statements about Jesus' healing ministry:

- ◆ Matthew 4:23–25 & Luke 6:17–19

◆   Matthew 8:16–17; Mark 1:32–34 & Luke 4:40
◆   Matthew 11:4–5 & Luke 7:21–22
◆   Matthew 9:35
◆   Matthew 12:15–16 & Mark 3:10–12
◆   Matthew 14:14; Luke 9:11 & John 6:2
◆   Matthew 14:34–36 & Mark 6:55–56
◆   Matthew 15:30–31
◆   Matthew 19:2
◆   Matthew 21:14
◆   Luke 5:15–16
◆   Luke 8:2.

From these passages, we can develop some principles about the healing ministry which are relevant for us. The incidents introduce us to around thirty people who were cured: twenty-four men, three women and three children. Obviously many more people were healed, but these are singled out by the Spirit as special examples for our instruction and edification.

Who does Jesus heal?
The Old Testament prophets are often reported as ministering God's healing to people in authority. The Gospels, however, describe Jesus focusing on ordinary people: in nineteen examples he serves people at the edge of society, and in the other eleven examples he ministers to ordinary people suffering from terrible afflictions.

What does Jesus heal?
The incidents record Jesus healing quadriplegia, paraplegia, a severed ear, a withered hand, blind eyes, leprous bodies, severe fevers, a gynaecological disorder, chronic curvature of the spine, dropsy, deafness and death. The general statements add that he healed epileptics, set lame people walking, dumb people talking, and made cripples whole. Matthew 4:23–36 summarises his ministry particularly well.

Jesus did not appear to focus on ministering to people with ailments which were merely inconvenient, or with matters which the medicine of his day could heal. Instead, he seemed to concentrate on serving people whose suffering caused isolation, loneliness, unemployment, or whose ailments had persisted for long periods of time.

Where does Jesus heal?
The general statements describe Jesus ministering healing in front of large crowds. We should note, however, that Jesus did not seek the crowds; the crowds sought him. They went to inconvenient locations at unsociable times, descended on homes where miracles had occurred, or gathered at the place where they knew Jesus to be.

As well as healing at these sorts of informal gatherings, Jesus also went to people and healed them wherever they were. Most of the ministry occurred when Jesus was on a journey. Four people were healed in their homes, one in a garden, another at a dinner party, one at his funeral, another in his grave, one at a house meeting, another at a pool, and two at regular services in the synagogue. Sometimes Jesus even healed at a long distance from the one who was sick.

How does Jesus initiate ministry?
In the Gospels, Jesus' healing ministry was always initiated in one of two different ways. He followed the pattern established by the Old Testament prophets and set an example which we do well to follow. In the New Testament, Jesus heals only in response to:

- ◆ Human requests – someone saying, 'Please heal me' or 'Please heal my friend/servant/child'
- ◆ Divine instruction – the Holy Spirit ordering, 'Go heal that person'.

In twelve incidents, the initiative was an unsought request by a friend, relative or the person themselves. In the other eight examples, the Spirit prompted Jesus to go to an individual and minister God's healing. Of course, the Gospels do not record

Jesus ministering healing to all the sick people in Israel, but they do make it clear that:

- ◆ He was always certain of the Father's willingness to heal
- ◆ He healed all those who came to him asking for healing
- ◆ He healed those who were identified to him by the Spirit.

How does Jesus minister healing?
We have seen that the Old Testament prophets either interceded for healing or announced the arrival of healing. The Gospels do not record Jesus interceding for healing, instead they show him restricting himself to doing just what he understood the Father to be doing. This seemed to vary with almost every example of the healing ministry.

Jesus' healings were performed without fanfare. When he was serving people in healing, the Gospels describe Jesus as usually using one or more of the following:

- ◆ Touch
- ◆ A spoken command of healing
- ◆ An announcement of healing.

The story of a woman who touched Jesus' garment stands out. Rather than Jesus touching her, she touched him – and he immediately noticed power leaving him. It seems that the healing anointing was so strong upon Jesus that the woman's faith was enough to appropriate it. She stretched out to Jesus, and God honoured her faith – which is what happens today when we reach out to him in faithful prayer.

What happens after Jesus ministers healing?
Jesus often gave helpful advice and reassurance *after* healing a person. We see this, for example, in Mark 5:43 & John 9:35–41.

Spectators or relatives are reported as being converted only in John 4:53. Twice we read that news of the miracle spread, once that people admired Jesus, and twice that they felt awe. In some cases, however, the reaction was negative: twice there was persecution, once there was argument, and another time plots of destruction. The chief priests determined to kill Jesus after the raising of Lazarus, and they seized him as their servant grew a new ear. Remarkably, in five instances, the Gospels report no reaction to Jesus' healing ministry.

Not all the people healed started to follow and believe in Jesus. Peter's mother-in-law served Jesus; the John 9 beggar worshipped him; the nobleman's son believed in him; Bartimeus was saved; but only one leper returned to Christ — the other nine stayed away.

The disciples' healing ministry

As part of his healing ministry, Jesus trained his disciples to continue his ministry after his ascension. First, he ensured that they were with him when he healed the sick; then, after they had spent many months watching him, Jesus invested them with his authority to cure the sick. They were given the right to speak in the power of Christ's own name.

Luke 8:22–9:6 describes Jesus' twelve apostles' first healing mission. Matthew 10:1–16; Mark 3:13–19 & Luke 9:1–6 list Jesus' detailed instructions, with Matthew identifying the pairs of apostles who worked together. After the mission, they returned to Jesus to give him an account of what had happened, and he withdrew with them to Bethsaida so that they could have time for prayer, rest and assessment.

Some time later, Jesus expanded his healing ministry to include a further seventy disciples. Again they were sent in pairs to definite locations, with the instruction to heal and preach the good news. The Gospels do not record any details from these trips, but Luke 9:40–41 suggests that the disciples were not always completely successful in healing the sick.

We can say that Jesus modelled and multiplied his healing ministry so that at least eighty disciples were involved. They served in pairs, using the authority of the name of Jesus. After his resurrection, Jesus urged them, in Acts 1:4–5 & Luke 24:49, to stay in Jerusalem until they received the prophet's anointing with the Holy Spirit for themselves.

Before Calvary, the disciples ministered as Gehazi had tried – using delegated prophetic authority. After Pentecost – when they were anointed with the Spirit – they served in the same way as Elisha and Jesus – as members of God's anointed, prophetic, healing community.

The book of Acts records eight examples of healing:

- ◆ The lame man at the temple gate – 3:1–10
- ◆ Blind Saul – 9:8–19
- ◆ Paralysed Aeneas – 9:32–35
- ◆ Dead Tabitha – 9:36–43
- ◆ The cripple at Lystra – 14:8–10
- ◆ Persecuted Paul – 14:19–20
- ◆ Eutychus – 20:7–12
- ◆ Publius' father – 28:7–8.

There are also seven general statements about the healing ministry: Acts: 2:43; 5:12–16; 6:8; 8:4–8; 14:3; 19:11–12 & 28:9. A careful reading shows that the New Testament disciples closely followed the general ministry principles of the Old Testament prophets and Christ.

Who do the disciples serve?
The people they ministered to were beggars, social outcasts, opponents of the gospel, friends, and an elderly relative of the Prefect of Malta.

What ailments do they heal?
Most of the people they ministered to suffered from long-standing, serious, socially disruptive and economically disabling diseases – for example, dysentery, death, paralysis and blindness.

Where do they minister?
In Acts, they ministered healing on the way to a prayer meeting, in a private house, during an informal open-air meeting, in a field after violent persecution, and at a church communion service.

How do they initiate healing ministry?
The general statements suggest that, like Jesus, the disciples ministered to all those who came requesting healing. And seven of the examples show that the believers were ready to minister when they recognised the Holy Spirit's prompting.

For example, we cannot know precisely how Peter was prompted to begin ministering in Acts 3:6, but in some way the Spirit informed him that the lame man was to be healed and that he was to speak the words. Peter 'felt' or 'heard' the Spirit's prompting, recognised that it was the Spirit and not his imagination or a demonic distraction, and obeyed God's voice by speaking and acting. God worked the miracle.

In Acts 9:10–19, Ananias' ministry was prompted by a vision, but God did not make him serve Saul. Once Ananias recognised that the thoughts he sensed were God's voice, it was a question of obedience. God would not work without his servant, and Ananias could not serve independently of God. This important story shows that healing ministry is not only for church leaders, but also for ordinary disciples.

Peter's encounter with Aeneas in Acts 9:32–35 does not appear to be anything other than regular pastoral visitation. As Peter stood over Aeneas, he sensed that God was about to cure the paralytic. Peter had been anointed with the Spirit at Pentecost, and this 'sensing' or prompting was God keeping his Amos 3:7–8 promise.

A similar pattern is followed in the other Acts examples of the healing ministry.

How do the disciples minister?
The examples suggest that the disciples often spoke words of command when they partnered God in his ministry. For example:

♦ Peter commanded: 'In the name of Jesus Christ of Nazareth, rise up and walk' – Acts 3:6

♦ Ananias announced: 'The Lord Jesus has sent me that you may receive your sight' – Acts 9:17

- ◆ Peter declared: 'Aeneas, Jesus Christ heals you; arise and make your bed' – Acts 9:34
- ◆ Peter ordered: 'Arise' Acts 9:40
- ◆ Paul called: 'Stand up straight on your feet' – Acts 14:10.

Only in Acts 28:8 do the disciples seem to use touch without a command or announcement of healing.

The general statements in Acts 5:12 & 19:11 are similar to the story of the woman who touched Jesus' garment. It seems that the faith which is implicit in this behaviour was honoured by God. Perhaps, also, the healing anointing was so strong upon Peter and Paul at these times that – as with Elisha's bones – it was almost something tangible.

What happens after ministry?
Acts reports that the disciples' healing ministry had a significant role in evangelism and early church growth. For example:

- ◆ After ministering to the lame man, Peter and John were arrested, imprisoned and reprimanded by the rulers; but many of those who heard Peter's explanation of the miracle became believers
- ◆ Ananias' service led to Paul's extremely effective ministry
- ◆ When Aeneas was healed, 'all who dwelt at Lydda and Sharon saw him and turned to the Lord'
- ◆ The whole of Joppa heard about Tabitha's resuscitation, 'and many believed on the Lord'.

Not all the incidents, however, describe a specific evangelistic impact. The healing of the cripple in Lystra led to misunderstanding and persecution. The people were 'greatly encouraged' by Eutychus' recovery, but nobody is reported as being saved. And many requested healing after Publius' father was cured, but Acts does not actually mention any conversions. This suggests, that healing is more than a 'tool for evangelism' but that it is a gracious and loving manifestation of God's mercy.

The contexts of healing ministry

When Jesus introduced himself as the fulfilment of Isaiah 61:1–2, he made it clear that he was concerned to serve the poor. Luke 4:18 is an important statement, which we can think of as Jesus' 'manifesto' or 'mission statement'. It summarises the purpose of his anointing with the Spirit as 'preaching the gospel to the poor', and provides five examples of what this means in practice.

This shows that 'healing' and 'releasing' (which we examine later) are not different activities to 'preaching the gospel to the poor', instead they are that preaching in action. It also suggests that anointed healing and releasing ministries should be set in several clear contexts.

A focus on the hurting

Many leaders disagree about the identity of 'the poor' whom Jesus was anointed to reach. The Greek word *ptochos* literally means 'someone who is cowering down or hiding for fear'. Some Bibles helpfully reflect this by referring to 'the afflicted' instead of 'the poor', and we can appreciate this today by thinking in terms of 'the hurting'.

This means that the Spirit's anointing is not given to help us reach mainly those who have few material or financial resources. Instead, the anointing is for helping people who are afflicted and hurting – those who are broken-hearted, blind, imprisoned, oppressed, and so on.

This helps us understand that 'preaching the gospel to the poor' does not mean restricting this ministry to one particular group of people, as if the gospel is only for the most destitute people in society. Instead, it means reaching out to the great mass of ordinary people around us who are afflicted, hurting and troubled.

A focus on the kingdom

In Part One of *The Rule of God*, we see how Jesus announced the coming of the kingdom with signs and wonders. The kingdom is God's heavenly rule breaking into the earthly realm, the powers of the 'age to come' invading this 'present evil age'. The kingdom of Satan is being pushed back by the kingdom of God (Matthew 11:12). The healings and miracles of Jesus are proof positive that the kingdom of God has come, as Matthew 12:28 shows.

Peter's description of Jesus ministry in Acts 10:38 makes this point clearly, '…how God anointed Jesus of Nazareth with the Holy Spirit and power, [and he] went about doing good and healing all who were oppressed by the devil, for God was with him.' The *message* of the kingdom and the *miracles* of the kingdom are the *manifestation* of the kingdom. The healing ministry of Jesus is, therefore, linked to the coming of the kingdom. Healings are 'signs' of the kingdom's presence because they are 'samples' of the kingdom's activity. In that respect they are God's 'shop window' on the kingdom. It is God's way of revealing his kingdom to the world.

A focus on evangelism

Luke 4:18 shows that Jesus was anointed with the Holy Spirit to reach the hurting by preaching the gospel. This means that ministry to the hurting should not be divorced from preaching the gospel to them.

We have seen that the prophets' anointing with the Spirit in the Old Testament fully equipped them for the healing ministry, but that their anointing was given principally to inspire and empower them to pass on the word of the Lord and call people back to God.

In the same way, Jesus' anointing was given for the main purpose of speaking God's words – but this involved healing and deliverance. Equally, the anointing with the Spirit which directs and empowers our ministry is also given so that we may make Jesus better known.

Jesus' healing ministry pointed to God's compassion and power, but it also confirmed what he said. His actions illustrated his announcing that the kingdom of God had come among ordinary people in great power, and that it was wide open to everyone.

The disciples Jesus trained were sent to proclaim the kingdom of God *and* to heal the sick *and* to release people from demons. These charges were inseparable. They went in pairs from village to village and served the people they met – by announcing the good news *and* by ministering God's healing *and* by releasing people from the grip of evil.

The early Christians kept these callings together. They preached and they healed and they cast out demons. When someone was healed or released, a spoken explanation was offered which pointed to Jesus. This was one of the main reasons for the church's phenomenal growth.

A relevant lifestyle
Jesus lived among ordinary hurting people in a way which showed that God accepted and loved them. His healing ministry both confirmed the good news that he taught about forgiveness, and also demonstrated the divine love that his living among them suggested.

He moved among the afflicted to preach the gospel and minister God's healing. He did not come from heaven with all the splendour and public acclaim to which, as God, he was entitled. Instead, he demonstrated his identification with humanity by living as an ordinary man, and by being subject to the same pressures as everyone else.

He lived in a way to which the hurting people of his day could relate. He ate their food, stayed in their homes, listened to their concerns, and was always available to them. He even befriended and identified with those who were rejected by ordinary society.

The anointed ministry of healing cannot be entirely removed from this context of 'living the gospel among the hurting' without some distortion of both the message and the ministry. This means that all our ministry in the Spirit should be set in the context of a lifestyle which facilitates the proclamation of the gospel by ensuring that we are focused on the afflicted, are relevant to their needs, and are personally accessible to them.

We also need to recognise that, in Luke 9:1–6 & 10:1–9, Jesus instructed his disciples to minister from within a lifestyle which depended on God for healing power *and* material provision.

The healing of believers

Most New Testament examples of the healing ministry are set in an evangelistic context, and this is reflected in passages like Mark 16:14–18. The New Testament, however, does not ignore all the Old Testament promises of healing which God has given to his people.

James 5:13–16 is an important passage on healing with a particular pastoral application. It encourages believers to ask God for their own healing – to believe God's promises and receive the healing they need from the Lord – and also to present themselves for pastoral healing.

5:13 teaches the correct response to suffering: we are meant to pray, not complain about our lot. We have to find our own resource in God, not depend on the experience or testimony of others.

We are not left on our own if the sickness persists. 5:14 states that we should then call for our pastoral leaders to minister to us.

5:15 teaches that the prayer of faith will heal the sick. The Greek word for 'heal', *sozo*, is used throughout the New Testament for both 'heal' and 'save'. This reminds us that healing is an aspect of God's wider work of salvation.

5:15 shows that it is not the oil which heals, nor the prayers of the leader, nor the faith of the believer – it is the Lord who raises up.

5:15 returns to the Old Testament principle that sin may be a cause of the sickness. Pastoral counselling is the solution, and the leaders must ensure that *mutual* confession takes place. We look at this later.

Ministry in the Spirit
Obviously, we have much to learn about the healing ministry from the New Testament, but a straightforward implementation of the pattern, procedures and contexts is inadequate.

Above all else, we need to receive the anointing of the Spirit without which we are as uninspired and impotent as Gehazi. Unless all our ministering is directed and empowered by the Holy Spirit, we are doomed to disappointment and ineffectiveness.

Part Six

The healing ministry today

We have seen that only a select few who had been anointed with the Holy Spirit – the prophets – were eligible for the healing ministry in the Old Testament. Since Jesus baptised the Church in the Holy Spirit at Pentecost, however, it has been possible for all believers to serve with God in his healing ministry. The only requirement is that we have been anointed by Jesus with the Holy Spirit.

The 'Great Commission' of Matthew 28:18–20 means that, to the end of time, *all* believers in *every* nation should be taught to obey *all* the instructions which Christ gave to the original twelve apostles. This must include his charge to heal the sick.

Of course, some believers will be more involved in healing than others. A few may receive a particular 'gift' of healing. But every member of God's prophetic people can minister his healing. This means that we should avoid styles of church services and models of ministry which give the impression that only a special few can minister healing.

Romans 12:6 states that we should use the gift of prophecy in proportion to our faith. This suggests that the gift can be more or less strongly developed in different people, or in the same person over a period of time. This seems to be why – in 1 Timothy 4:14 & 2 Timothy 1:6 – Timothy was reminded not to neglect the gift he had and to rekindle it within him.

If it was possible for Timothy to allow his gift to weaken, perhaps through infrequent use, so it is surely similar for us in relation to healing. And if Timothy's gift can be strengthened by using it, so we should develop all the spiritual and practical skills necessary for effective ministry.

In particular, we need to gain experience and expertise in the spiritual gifts which are important for ministering Christian healing with God. As well as knowing that the Father is the healing God, and that the Son heals, and that the Spirit is in us and with us to heal, we also need to grasp the 'how to' of ministering in healing.

God's prompting to minister

We have seen that all ministry in the Spirit hinges on recognising the promptings and directings of the Spirit. We may know all the biblical principles and promises, but we will not be able to minister effectively until we recognise how God communicates with us through the Spirit.

We have seen that the Old Testament prophets were inspired to speak and to serve by the Word of God, the burden of the Lord, and the Spirit of God – and we can expect to be directed in a similar way.

God does speak to us quietly over a period of time, preparing us to serve with him. But he also speaks to us when he wants us to minister, and this is generally through what has come to be known as the spiritual gift of 'words of knowledge'.

We have seen that Jesus and the apostles 'sensed' that God wanted them to minister to a particular person, and – with the Spirit's help – they identified that person in a crowd. For example, Jesus ministered to only one man at the pool of Bethesda, and Peter knew that God wanted him to minister to the lame man at the Temple gate.

Likewise today, we can become aware in our spirit that God is healing people or is about to heal people. For example, we may 'sense' some sort of description of either the person or the condition that God is going to heal.

Sometimes, when ministering healing, people receive a visual impression of the person who is being healed, or – on other occasions – they may 'feel' a pain, a warmth or some other sensation in the relevant part of their own bodies. These are some of the Spirit's ways of indicating that God is healing a condition.

Recognising God's will to minister
Knowing God's will can be one of the hardest parts of the Christian life, but the basic principles of discipleship and listening to God apply in every aspect of serving God, including ministry in the Spirit. It is just as important for us to listen to the Spirit and be guided and enabled by him when we take someone a meal as when we cast out a demon. However we are led to serve or minister, we must be directed by him.

Asking God specific questions is probably the best way of learning to identify his voice. First, we need to ask God what we should do or say; next, we 'sieve' or test the thoughts that come to separate the human dross from the bits which are purely divine; and then we put the tested conclusion into practice. We examine this whole area in *Listening to God*.

Starting to minister God's healing

The suggestions here, and similar ones in later chapters for other areas of ministry, are not biblical rules to follow slavishly, rather they are guidelines which the Spirit should be asked to interpret and apply to different situations.

Prayer
Lack of adequate preparatory prayer is one of the main reasons for the ineffectiveness of ministry. At least an equal amount of time should be spent in prayer as we anticipate spending in ministry. This should include intercession for boldness, as in Acts 4:29–30, and silent listening waiting for God's prompting about ministry, as in Acts 9:40.

Partnership
We have seen that the theme of partnership runs through the Bible. This suggests that we should normally minister healing in pairs or a team. The disciples learnt from being with Jesus when he healed, so it is good preparation and training for us to join with another believer who is more experienced. In *Glory in the Church*, we see how the cell system can enhance the discipleship process in church life. The same is true of

ministering in the Spirit. Your cell is the place where you can learn to minister and the small group that can provide both the example and support for you as you step out into this new area with the Spirit.

It is best to avoid having more than three people ministering to one person, as this can be confusing and ineffective, as seems to be the case in Matthew 17:16. Other believers who are eager to be involved in service can sit quietly and unobtrusively, whilst engaging in urgent prayer for the empowering and guidance of those ministering.

Patience
2 Corinthians 6:3–4 shows that ministers need much patience, as we are quickly drained by delays, problems and difficult people.

The Bible uses different Greek words for 'patience towards people', *makrothumia*, and 'patience towards circumstances', *hupomone*; and teaches different things about them. Older versions of the Bible reflect this by generally translating *makrothumia* as 'long-suffering'.

We do not need to pray for *makrothumia*, as we have Jesus' patience towards people within us. We see this in Galatians 3:27 & Colossians 3:12. Galatians 5:22 indicates that this type of patience develops naturally within us as one aspect of the Spirit's work in our lives.

The Bible suggests, however, that we should ask for *hupomone* or 'staying power' – which, in 2 Corinthians 12:12, is a sign of an apostle. James 1:2–4 shows that God develops this in us through our testing, training and suffering. We need *hupomone* to stop circumstances from dictating our response in ministry, and to help us persevere when discouragement comes.

Humility
Some believers are attracted to the healing ministry for wrong reasons. Compassion and obedience motivated Christ, and we should seek the humble, self-effacing anonymity of the Holy Spirit – aiming to focus all attention upon God without basking in any associated glory.

No human can ever heal another. The most that we can aim for is to be an 'unprofitable' servant whom God advises in advance of a miracle.

Questions
We have noted that the scriptural initiative for healing ministry was either someone requesting, 'Please heal me' or God commanding, 'Minister my healing to that person'. The split in the New Testament healing miracles is exact: half are in response to divine instruction and half to human request.

In ministry, we need to listen both to God and to the person we are seeking to help, and this is facilitated by creating a climate of quiet and privacy. Time and again, the Gospels show how Jesus silenced noise or moved into a private place before commencing ministry.

Jesus did not function only at a supernatural level, but also at the natural level of observation and deduction. Mark 5:9, 8:22–26; 9:14–29; Luke 18:40–43 & John 5:6 report him asking five obvious questions. We will often need to ask similar questions.

◆　'What is your name?'
Jesus may have addressed this question to a demon, but – for us – it is a natural question to put to a stranger.

◆　'What do you want me to do?'
This helps the person to be clear in their own minds about what they are seeking.

◆　'Do you want to be well?'
It is helpful to check both that the person is serious and aware of the consequences of healing, and also that we are not trying to 'force' healing on them.

◆　'How long has this been happening?'
The circumstances and background of the problem may need to be investigated to clarify the cause of the sickness.

◆　'Can you see?'
We should always try to establish what has happened during the ministry.

As well as questioning the person, we should ask God whether anything else needs to be known. We may 'sense' a picture or word to pass on. We may 'be aware' of a question or a non-physical cause. If God tells us nothing, the person has told us all we need to know.

The physical conditions of Abimelech, Miriam, Malchus, the man at the pool of Bethesda and the man let down through the roof appear to have had their origin in sin. Some leaders today would insist on repentance and forgiveness before admitting any possibility of healing, but this is not the biblical pattern. At times, as in James 5:16, there is an association between the confession of sin and pastoral healing, but this is not always the case.

Other leaders teach that a demon lies behind every disease, and demand that it is cast out before healing can begin. As we will see later, the Bible distinguishes between deliverance from demons and physical healing. This distinction needs constant emphasis.

Ministry

We have noted the different healing actions used by Jesus and the disciples, and we would do well to follow their example. We should remember, however, three general scriptural principles.

- ◆ 'Laying hands' on the head is associated more with the ministry of blessing than with healing – we consider this in Part Ten.

- ◆ Prayer takes place before ministry: words of command or announcement accompany healing ministry.

- ◆ God may prompt us to suggest an action for the person to perform.

The following suggestions are for believers who are inexperienced in the healing ministry. They should be varied as the Holy Spirit guides us along his own path of action.

- ◆ Show Christ's love at all times; smile and relax, for God is the healer.

◆ Together with a partner, quietly confess any sins and seek forgiveness.

◆ Ask the Holy Spirit to give you guidance, boldness and power. Seek him for direction on how to pray – try to discern whether to pray a prayer of petition, agreement, etc. or whether to speak a word of command, pronouncement or rebuke.

◆ Keep your eyes open; helpful information is often received by watching the person's reactions.

◆ Listen to God and speak whatever he puts into your mind; keep on asking him questions and listening to his replies.

◆ Ask God whether the person should be touched; if prompted, gently place a hand on the clothing nearest to the affected part of the body. Always ask the person's permission before touching them.

◆ Ask questions like, 'What is happening?' and 'Do you feel anything?' Ensure they let you know what is happening to them.

◆ Watch out for bodily reactions; these may indicate that God is at work, but they are only the body's natural response to God's work.

◆ If a bodily reaction occurs, help the person to be comfortable, but press on with the ministry.

◆ Encourage the person and help them relax; remind them of the presence, power and promises of God.

◆ Maintain a flow of ministry with the person, your partner, and God.

◆ When unsure what to do next, it may be helpful to pray in tongues; explain to the person what this is.

◆ Stop ministering when the person is healed, or the Holy Spirit says stop, or you cannot think of anything else to do, or the person asks you to stop, or when anyone appears tired.

- ◆ If the person believes that they have been healed, or feels that something has happened in their body, get them to check it out there and then if it is possible. If appropriate, ask them to do something they were unable to do before the healing.
- ◆ If the person is not fully healed, arrange to minister again in the near future, allowing time for further preparation and prayer.

Aftercare

We have seen that Jesus often passed on his Father's advice, or direction, after he had ministered to a person. We can follow his example and offer whatever practical advice the Spirit prompts us to give. For example, he might ask us to mention some of the following matters:

- ◆ The person can be encouraged to offer praise and thanksgiving
- ◆ When drugs have been prescribed, or the person has been receiving special medical care, they should be urged to visit their doctor
- ◆ Point them towards the next step in Christian commitment – whether repentance, baptism, receiving the Spirit or joining a church
- ◆ If the cause of the ailment was sin, or if there was a demonic element, this should be recognised and renounced
- ◆ Further ministry will sometimes be necessary; explain this and make the appropriate arrangements
- ◆ Pray for their continuing healing, safety and protection; the enemy has been defeated, but he must be expected to fight back.

Ministry to the unhealed

We have noted that Jesus healed everyone who requested healing, and cured all those to whom the Father sent him. But the rest of the New Testament is not a catalogue of unbroken success. Galatians 4:13–14; Philippians 2:27; 1 Timothy 5:23 & 2 Timothy 4:20 may imply either unsuccessful or unattempted ministry for healing.

All believers who commit themselves to the ministry of healing will face some disappointment. There will be some people we help who are not healed, others whose initial healing lapses, and a few who are half-healed and then make no further progress.

Sometimes, this will be because the cure of our pride was higher on God's agenda. In other instances we will have misheard God or will have acted out of human enthusiasm or because of worldly or human pressure. And there will be times when we have not prayed enough or have been distracted by materialism or unnecessary worries.

Sadly, some believers imply – either by innuendo or out of embarrassment – that ineffective ministry is the responsibility of the one they served. They hint that the person did not have enough faith, or was a little rebellious, or did not really want to be completely healed. All these are possible, but they are rarely the truth.

Sometimes, as with many of the Old Testament stories, the appreciation of the healing is delayed. At other times the actual healing is gradual – as with Naaman, and the blind man in Mark 8. In cases like these, however, there is no scriptural authority for ever suggesting that anyone should be urged to pretend that they are healed. The people in these stories were simply asked to obey God's word to them.

We must recognise that there is no biblical record of Christ informing anyone that they could not be healed because *they* lacked enough faith or belief. Matthew 13:58 & 17:19–20 teach quite different truths.

When – after much ministry – an expected cure has not taken place, we can do some of the following things. As with the other suggestions, we should ask God to shape them to our situation.

◆ Have a debriefing with your ministry partner and go through the steps taken in ministry. Try and find out whether you were obedient to every prompting; establish whether any mistakes or omissions were made.

◆ Pray and fast for guidance; ask God why the person was not healed.

◆ Talk and pray about the matter with someone who is more experienced in the healing ministry, and ask for their suggestions.

◆ Praise God with the person for the time spent together; remind them that the healing God is with them and cares for them.

◆ Establish what was learnt from the episode and explain this to the person. Find out what they learnt through the ministry, and praise God together for any insights.

◆ If the person being helped is a believer, encourage them to join in healing prayer for others.

◆ Remember that we are part of a battle, that the enemy is implacably opposed to healing, but that he was defeated on the cross and will be destroyed at the last day.

◆ Make sure that nobody feels guilty about the lack of healing.

◆ Encourage the person to meditate on God's biblical healing promises and to apply them to their situation.

Although we should urge people to go on praying for their healing, and to claim God's promises for healing, we should not neglect to remind them to be hungrier for the healer than their healing. Healing, ultimately, is not the great hope of humanity. Jesus is.

In the middle of all our pain and problems, our only hope of inner peace and contentment is to keep our attention tightly focused on Jesus – and on his overwhelming love for us. If we are pre-occupied with healing, we will never be whole and we will never know peace. But if our goal is God himself, we will find that *Yahweh Rapha* soon embraces us in his gentle healing arms.

Part Seven

The basis of deliverance ministry

A second obvious way that Jesus serves individuals is by releasing or delivering them from evil powers. Before we examine the way that he ministers through casting out demons, we need to appreciate that this is part of the wider biblical teaching about God's deliverance ministry.

Deliverance from sin

We have noted Acts 10:38, and have recognised that Jesus was anointed with the Holy Spirit and with power and that, as a result, he healed all who were oppressed by the devil. This shows us that people really can be oppressed in some way by the devil, and that deliverance ministry is a significant feature of Jesus' ministry in the Spirit.

In recent years, there has been some controversy about 'deliverance ministry' and much of this has been based in the way that different groups of believers use words like 'exorcism' and 'possession', and 'name' personalised or individual demons. The New Testament, however, does not lay down categories of oppression by the enemy. Instead, it calls us to fix our eyes on Jesus and to stamp our feet on all the works of the enemy.

Also, nowadays in some Christian circles there is much speculation as to what demons – often called evil or unclean spirits – really are and how they actually originated. Are they fallen angels associated with Satan's rebellion or are they disembodied members of a pre-Adamic race? Should we make a distinction between *daimon* and its derivative *daimonion*, Greek words which most English Bibles simply translate as 'demon'?

Though these – and others – are of course interesting questions, their answers must unfortunately remain just theories as the biblical data – what little that there is on such issues – can be interpreted varyingly. This means we must exercise caution when entertaining such questions and be careful not to read in too much on issues that the Bible sees fit not to comment on. Ultimately, God is passionate about people and the state of their lives and this is why the Scriptures concentrate more on the effects of demons in human lives than on any classification or detailed description of demons.

Ephesians 6:12 shows that there are different types of demonic powers – much as there are angels, archangels, *cherubim* and *seraphim* – but the Bible is more interested in teaching us to resist the enemy than in helping us to define him.

For example, although the Bible does refer to *a spirit of jealousy*, Numbers 5:14; *a spirit of prostitution*, Hosea 5:4; *a spirit of infirmity*, Luke 13:11; *a spirit of slavery*, Romans 8:15; and *a spirit of timidity*, 2 Timothy 1:7, the focus in these passages is on the results of demonic activity in people's lives rather than on the demon itself. Passages like these are rather similar to the way that the Scriptures refer to the Holy Spirit in verses like Isaiah 11:2; Zechariah 12:10; John 14:17; Romans 8:15 & 1 Peter 4:15. They are lovely descriptions of aspects of his work, rather than careful attempts to define him fully.

Demons undoubtedly can cause and contribute to every form of evil and sin. They do want to bring about, for example, jealousy, prostitution, infirmity, slavery and timidity. But we must concentrate more on God and his release than on the demons doing the afflicting; and we must try to learn from the Scriptures how we can resist the devil, how God frees people, and how we can minister to people who need to be released or delivered.

God's ministry of forgiveness is by far the most important aspect of his deliverance ministry, for forgiveness is deliverance from sin – it is deliverance from the very grip of Satan. Although many people do need to be released from demonic oppression, a right understanding and appropriation of the Father's forgiveness, together with a firm resolution to sin no more, are all the ministry that most people need to release them from their problem.

Sin
The most common Greek word for sin is *hamartia*. This is sometimes used to describe sinful acts, but is more commonly used to mean the state of sinfulness. It describes the irresistible inner moral power which controls people. *Hamartia* means the disobedience which cannot say 'yes' to God and brings about nonconformity to his standards.

Hamartia affects our relationship with God. Until we are delivered from slavery to sin, we are eternally alienated from God. When the biblical material about sin is read – Romans 7, for example – it is easy to understand why some people in its grip think that they need to have a demon cast out.

Three other Greek words are also used for sin in the New Testament.

◆ *Paraptoma* is used, for example, in Romans 4:25; 5:15 & Ephesians 2:1. It is usually translated as 'trespass' and means an unpremeditated fault. It emphasises the thoughtless, careless nature of sin.

◆ *Parabasis* is used in Romans 2:23; 5:14; Galatians 3:19 & 1 Timothy 2:14. It is a stepping aside, a deliberate deviation from the true path, and is normally translated as 'transgression'. It stresses the wilful, deliberate side of sin.

◆ *Anomia* is used in Matthew 23:28; 24:12 & 2 Corinthians 6:14. It means lawlessness or iniquity, and refers to the opposite of whatever is right and good. It shows that sin is exactly the opposite of God.

These three words convey the idea of failing to match God's perfect requirements, and they describe deeds and attitudes which separate us from each other and from God. Although the words are largely synonymous, their different shades of meaning help us understand the subtle and complex nature of sin.

Initial forgiveness from sin
The Bible promises forgiveness for all aspects of sin; for *hamartia*, Colossians 1:14; *paraptoma*, Colossians 2:13; *parabasis*,

Hebrews 9:15; and *anomia*, Titus 2:14. The common contemporary understanding of forgiveness, however, is so weak that the full breadth of meaning of biblical forgiveness is rarely appreciated and enjoyed. Three concepts are involved with God's initial forgiveness.

◆ Initial forgiveness from sin means that God remits the punishment due to the presence of sin and removes the barrier which exists between himself and each member of humanity. We can call this 'deliverance from the penalty – or wages – of sin'.

◆ Initial forgiveness from sin means that God removes the offence and erases its memory. He covers over the deeds done – blots them out – so that they cannot be seen or remembered by him again. This is 'deliverance from the guilt of sin' and was promised in Jeremiah 31:31–34. These two aspects of initial forgiveness are foreshadowed in Leviticus 16 by the sacrifice of two goats.

◆ But it is the third element of initial forgiveness which is vital for our study of deliverance ministry. The teaching in Romans 6 of 'death to sin' expresses this forgiveness in a most dynamic form. The very life of the sin force is destroyed in a spiritual operation which removes *hamartia* – the moral compulsion to do wrong, the inability to comply with God's will. This is 'deliverance from the power of sin', and this is why Colossians 1:13–14 calls forgiveness 'our freedom'.

It is this vibrant, personal experience of God's initial forgiveness which *usually* renders casting out a demon unnecessary. Biblical forgiveness, when mixed with repentance, faith and water baptism, is *normally* adequate to release an individual from the power that Satan holds, through sin, on their life. We will see, however, that some people have become so afflicted and oppressed by demonic beings, that further deliverance is necessary.

The biblical emphasis on believers being 'delivered' from the power of sin means that the existence of sin in a believer's life must be considered a very serious matter. The continuing presence of sin in someone who has been delivered from the power of sin must expose them to possible demonic influence.

As deliverance from sin's power is such a powerful and important truth, the devil has a vested interest in trying to keep us ignorant and disbelieving of our true position in Christ. We can be sure that his demons are always trying both to make us fall back into sin, and to be convinced that we are not free from sin.

God's initial forgiveness is so powerful and all-embracing that it should be a central feature of all deliverance ministry. This means that we must understand how it is received. There are four aspects:

1. Free gift

Initial forgiveness – deliverance from the penalty, guilt and power of sin – is received as a free gift by those people who have believed in the Lord Jesus, have begun to turn their backs on the world, the flesh and the devil, and have firmly set their face towards God. Luke 15:11–32 & Acts 5:31 point to the grace involved.

2. Accomplished by Christ's blood

Many people ask why, if God already knew he would grant forgiveness, he could not dispense with the horror of Calvary and announce, like the father to the prodigal son, 'I forgive you.' But such a question reveals a low view of sin, forgiveness and God's holiness.

Sin must be removed before a holy God can allow reconciliation with humanity polluted by sin, and the Old Testament establishes the principle that sin can be removed only by the shedding of the blood of one without fault or blemish. On the cross, the sinless Christ shed his blood to deliver us from the filth of sin. Ephesians 1:4–7 explains God's plan.

83

At Calvary, Christ delivered us from the punishment of sin by voluntarily accepting the blame, enduring the agony of separation, taking the faults of many, and winning eternal redemption – as Hebrews 9–10 makes plain. And it was there that Christ delivered us from the power of sin, as Romans 6:9–11 powerfully underlines.

3. Received by faith

Although forgiveness is a free gift from God, there is nothing mechanical or automatic about it. It is not inevitable. Something has to be done before it can be experienced. Acts 26:18 asserts that Paul was sent to the Gentiles so they might receive initial forgiveness of sins 'through faith in Christ'. Through faith in Christ, we experience – we personally receive – what Christ has accomplished by his blood.

Acts 2:38; 3:26 & 10:43 show that there must be a human response to God's initiative. God has provided initial forgiveness through Christ's death, but this forgiveness is available only to those who turn decisively away from their sins and begin to believe and trust in Jesus.

4. Confirmed in baptism

The New Testament view of baptism always connects it with the atoning death of Christ and the forgiveness won by Christ. We see this, for example, in Acts 2:38 and 22:16.

God may not tie his gifts to any particular rite, but every repentant believer who is baptised in the name of Jesus Christ can expect to experience the immediate forgiveness of their sins. We consider this more fully in Part Ten of *Glory in the Church*.

The two Old Testament foreshadowings of baptism are clear acts of deliverance: there is a death to the old life in the great flood, and an end to slavery in the parting of the Red Sea. And Romans 6 teaches that, in baptism, God accomplishes a real element of deliverance from the old ways of life.

Initial forgiveness is unconditional, and nobody can do anything to earn it. However, the freedom must be received by faith in Christ and confirmed in baptism – only then can it be fully experienced.

This is a freedom which makes it possible for us to comply with God's will; a deliverance which brings freedom of choice where before no such choice existed; an escape from slavery to sin into God's own kingdom. Christian believers are the only beings on earth who can choose whether or not to sin. Passages like I John 3:5–9 make sense only when we appreciate the power of God's delivering forgiveness.

This has two important implications for us: it shows that baptism is an aspect of deliverance ministry; and it suggests that failure to be baptised could mean incomplete deliverance from demonic influence.

In some parts of the church, this is taken so seriously that baptism is a pre-condition for 'casting out' ministry.

Ongoing forgiveness
God's free gift of 'initial' forgiveness means that we need no longer live in habitual sin – for the power of sin has been broken. But we know that sin still lingers on, though not as master of our lives. Isolated acts of sin, as opposed to continual patterns of sin, occur.

In Greek, I John 3:6, 9 & 5:18 use the present tense to signify that continual sinning has ceased to exist in the forgiven believer, whereas I John 2:1 uses a different Greek construction – the aorist tense – to show that specific acts of sin arc still possible.

I John 1:8 shows that believers who say they never commit a single sin deceive themselves, and I John 5:14–17 makes it plain that Christians can still sin. I John 1:9; 2:1 & 5:16, however, promise 'ongoing' forgiveness and deliverance for isolated acts of sin which are committed after the initial experience of forgiveness has been received in faith and sealed in baptism.

85

No modern believer had committed any sins when Jesus died, for we were not alive. But God in his omniscience knew every sin that we would commit, and in Christ on the cross he dealt with them all. When we received his forgiveness, it was not only for all sin committed up to that moment, but for all future sin too. His gift of 'initial' forgiveness tore down the barrier between us and God, and – no matter what we do or fail to do – that barrier will not be re-erected.

One way of distinguishing between 'initial' and 'ongoing' forgiveness is by thinking of them as 'judicial' and 'parental' forgiveness. Judicial forgiveness is the forgiveness of justification which is eternal life, whereas parental forgiveness is the forgiveness of fellowship with God as our Father – it is what we see in the parable of the Prodigal Son.

The issue of our heavenly future is eternally settled by judicial forgiveness, but the extent to which we enjoy eternal life now and in heaven is determined by how we live.

True biblical preaching of the gospel of grace should always cause listeners to ask the Romans 6:1 question. No matter what a person does after they have experienced 'initial' forgiveness they still possess eternal life. However, our post-forgiveness sins destroy our earthly enjoyment of that eternal life, wreak havoc with our human relationships, reduce our heavenly rewards, hinder our sense of God's forgiveness and freedom from sin, and expose us to demonic influence. We need these sins to be dealt with by God's ongoing forgiveness – and some believers may also need another form of deliverance ministry.

Although initial or judicial forgiveness is always unconditional, ongoing or parental forgiveness for believers seems to have two conditions attached.

◆ Confession to God
1 John 1:8–9 deals with our need for 'ongoing' forgiveness, shows that our confession should be made directly to God, and implies that repentance should be involved throughout the Christian life.

This regular acknowledgement, or confession, of sin is a condition for ongoing forgiveness and maintains our intimate relationship with our Father.

◆   Forgiveness of others
Matthew 6:12–15; Luke 17:4 & Ephesians 4:32 stress that the basic human response to God's initial forgiveness should be an eagerness to forgive others.

We receive God's forgiveness so that we can forgive others in a similar way – we do not earn his forgiveness by forgiving others. Forgiving other people follows on from God's forgiveness and, as with human confession, deals primarily with faults, blunders and human relationships.

When Matthew 18:23–25 is taken with Matthew 6:14–15 & Mark 11:25, we can see that forgiveness of others springs from God first forgiving us, and that those who do not forgive others cease to enjoy God's forgiveness *on earth*: this works itself out in spoilt human relationships. Matthew 18:34 also suggests that this unforgiveness can expose us to demonic 'torturing'.

The implications of the biblical teaching on 'deliverance from sin' for the wider ministry of deliverance are clearly considerable. If the power of God in forgiveness is as great as the Bible suggests, then those ministering deliverance and those seeking deliverance can confidently seek God's all-delivering forgiveness as the first, and *probably* the only, stage on the journey to total freedom.

Deliverance from temptation
In Part Eight we will be studying how to deliver someone from a demon, but first we must look at the tactics Satan uses to ensnare people – it is crucial that these are not overlooked. Most believers are aware of the activity of evil forces, but few learn to ensure that preventative spiritual medicine is more prominent than corrective spiritual surgery.

Some believers appear to be so conscious of the devil and his demons that they forget they have the power of the Spirit to resist him; while others are so convinced he is a medieval myth that they do not bother to renounce him.

It is not always clear, as in Isaiah 14 & Ezekiel 28, whether some of the scriptural material about Satan is parabolic or literal, but it is always relevant – for the biblical accounts of his dealings with men and women teach us much about the ministry of deliverance.

Four Old Testament characters were tempted by Satan himself – not just by a demon. In each incident, Satan used a different weapon, attacked different aspects of the individuals' lives, and appeared in a different disguise with a different objective. These stories provide an overall picture of his evil strategy, and form a helpful foundation for our understanding of God's work of deliverance from temptation.

Eve

In Genesis 3, Satan appeared to Eve as a *deceiver*, misleading her about the nature of true human happiness – we also see him in this guise in Revelation 12:9. He attacked Eve's mind, using the weapon of lies, with the objective of making her ignorant of God's will.

In 3:1, Satan brought confusion by suggesting that Eve should doubt God's goodness, inferring that God must be bad if he sought to restrict legitimate pleasures like tasting the fruit he had just provided. This was a lie, as Eve pointed out, for God had not prohibited the consumption of fruit from every tree.

Satan tried to provoke Eve into questioning God's word, then, in 3:5, more lies were targeted on Eve's mind. These sowed the seeds of ambition which smothered her knowledge of God's will.

Satan still tries to deceive people about the nature of true happiness, and deliverance from this strategy is only by the Word of God. When Satan attacked Jesus with lies and ambition, it was this weapon of the Word of God which Jesus used to defeat his enemy: three times in Matthew 4:1–11, Christ told the devil, 'Scripture says'.

In Genesis 3:3, Eve used God's word to fight off her first attack, but neglected to use it again, yielded to the temptation, and sinned.

Job

The devil came as a *destroyer*, using the weapon of suffering to attack Job's body and make him pity himself and blame God for the evil.

God held Job up to Satan as an example of a virtuous servant. Satan replied that Job worshipped God only because of his wealth and divine protection. So God allowed Satan to test Job to see if he would remain faithful. Job 1:21–22 describes Job's response to the attack.

God pointed to Job's continued blamelessness, but Satan asserted that this would change if Job's body was affected. So God placed Job in Satan's power, and Satan attacked Job's body with sickness.

Satan did not employ suffering as an end in itself, but as a weapon to make Job turn against God. Satan wanted Job to slander God's name and attribute the evil to him. After seven days of silence, Job 3 records Job's terrible, 'Why?'

Deliverance from this satanic strategy is by the grace of God strengthening our human endurance and patience – as we see in Romans 8:18 & Colossians 1:24. Our faith in God's goodness must continue, even when we do not understand why the evil one is buffeting our bodies, our families and our circumstances.

1 Peter 5:8–11 shows that Satan still tries to destroy believers through suffering. God does not promise always to deliver us immediately from suffering, but he does promise to be with us, to strengthen us, and to free us from the snare of turning our back on him.

David

1 Chronicles 21 records the third biblical encounter with Satan. This time Satan appeared as a *despotic ruler* and attacked David's will with the weapon of pride. His aim was to cause the king to exercise authority independently of God's will. Satan incited David to take a census and, despite the opposition of Joab, this was carried out.

Ministers can deliver people by the score. Then, like David, they can be tempted by the prince of this world, John 12:31, into counting the scores as an act of pride – and so need deliverance themselves.

Deliverance from this strategy comes by unceasing openness to that member of the trinity who does not draw attention to himself, but lives to focus all glory upon another. When we are truly full of the Holy Spirit we do not boast about *our* numbers.

Joshua

In Zechariah 3, Satan came as a *defamer* and attacked the High Priest's conscience with self-condemnation. Satan's aim was to lead Joshua into a wrong sense of guilt at falling short of God's will, and he did this by tempting the priest to think that his dirty clothes disqualified him from service.

This is a still a common strategy of the defamer. He whispers a temptation in one ear, then skips around to accuse us in the other ear of having wrong thoughts! He brings constant reminders of past failings, long-forgiven sins, and a general sense of disqualification, defilement, inadequacy and unfitness for ministry.

Deliverance is not from falling short of God's will, but from self-condemnation – through the knowledge that Christ's blood has delivered us from God's condemnation. We see this deliverance by justification by God's grace in Zechariah 3:4–5.

All believers live in the tension between our awareness of our own faults and our understanding that we are justified by God. Once Satan has deadened our sense of justification by God, he can magnify our awareness of our faults, accuse us with constant reminders of them, and paralyse us with self-condemnation.

An anointed believer who is experienced in ministry can become utterly condemned by a failure or fault. Most of us still hear the same demonic whispers as Joshua, 'God can't use you because...'; 'Nothing is happening is because...'; 'Supposing everybody knew that...?'

Romans 8:38–39 shows that nothing – not even a demon or Satan – can come between us and God's love. But they can delude us into thinking that we have been separated from him. And many believers end up living as if they are separated from his love.

To resist these satanic strategies, we must constantly stress the priority of the Word of God, the grace of God, the Spirit of God and the sacrifice of God. They are the only sure basis for serving with Christ in his ministry of deliverance.

Part Eight

Deliverance in the New Testament

I John 3:8 teaches that Jesus came to undo all Satan had accomplished in corrupting and controlling God's creation, especially through sin. Jesus' ministry brought deliverance to humanity in general and to people as individuals – deliverance from every aspect of Satan's work.

Jesus' life, teaching and ministry fulfilled his Luke 4:18 manifesto, and this climaxed in his supreme act of deliverance. At Calvary, as Hebrews 2:14 –15 describes, Jesus defeated Satan and the power of death, and released those who were held captive.

Jesus cast out demons

To limit Christ's ministry of deliverance to the cross, however, is to ignore an important aspect of his earthly ministry. As well as feeding the hungry, healing the sick and preaching the good news, the Gospels show that Christ also released many people from the grip of evil forces.

Of course, it misrepresents the New Testament to suggest that casting out demons was Jesus' main ministry activity. As illustrations of his deliverance ministry in the Spirit, however, the Gospels record eight incidents when Jesus cast out evil spirits.

The expression, 'casting out demons' is rather clumsy, and many leaders have replaced it with 'deliverance'. We have seen, however, that deliverance is a general biblical term which includes deliverance from sin and temptation. Because of this, it is better to carry on using 'casting out demons'; though clumsy, it cannot be misunderstood.

The eight gospel incidents of casting out a demon or demons are:

- The Capernaum demoniac – Mark 1:21 & Luke 4:31–37
- Peter's mother-in-law – Matthew 8:14–15; Mark 1:29–31 & Luke 4:38–39
- The blind and dumb demoniac – Matthew 12:22–29 & Luke 11:14–22
- The Gadarene demoniacs – Matthew 8:28; Mark 5:1–20 & Luke 8:26–39
- The Canaanite's daughter – Matthew 15:21–28 & Mark 7:24–30
- The epileptic demoniac – Matthew 17:14–21; Mark 9:14–29 & Luke 9:37–43
- The crippled woman – Luke 13:10–17
- The dumb demoniac – Matthew 9:32–34.

There are also ten general statements about casting out evil powers:

- Matthew 4:24
- Matthew 8:16
- Mark 1:32–34
- Mark 1:39
- Mark 3:11
- Mark 6:13
- Luke 4:41
- Luke 6:18
- Luke 7:21
- Luke 11:24–26.

A careful reading of these incidents and general statements suggests eight basic principles about Jesus' ministry of casting out demons.

1. Jesus delivered people who were brought to his attention
We have seen that Jesus ministered healing when he was asked to do so by the sufferer or their representative, and when he was directly and immediately sent to a sick person by the Holy Spirit. The general statements indicate that, when Jesus was ministering deliverance, he successfully released all those who were brought to him needing help.

It is the same in the incidents. We see, for example, that the blind and dumb demoniac and Peter's mother-in-law were both released as a result of their being brought to Jesus by another. And the Capernaum demoniac brought himself to Jesus: his shrieks, cries and personal presence made it impossible for Jesus to ignore his plight.

The Gospels also record that Jesus went directly to a man to initiate this ministry. Mark 5:2–8 & Luke 8:26–29 seems to imply that Jesus sailed to the country of Gadarenes specifically to minister to the man. It surely cannot be a coincidence that Jesus landed on the Gadarene coast at the precise spot where there was a man who needed to be released from demons. The tense used in both passages suggests that Jesus had been ordering the demons to go even before he met the man.

The case of the crippled woman is less straightforward. The physical consequence of Satan's grip was visible to all who saw her, but it must have been the Spirit who showed Jesus that a demon was behind the physical condition. It is not clear, though, whether Jesus was motivated to release her by his compassion on seeing her, the fact that it was the Sabbath, the Spirit's prompting, or a combination of these.

We can say that Jesus cast out demons when he was asked by a representative of the sufferer, when a demon reacted to his presence, and when he was led to a sufferer by the Spirit. This does not mean we can *never* minister outside these conditions; but we should take Jesus' example very seriously – especially as it seems to apply in every aspect of his ministry.

2. Jesus asked few questions
Some leaders insist that the reason why a condition arose must be established before ministry can begin, while others stress the need for extensive diagnostic questioning and lengthy sessions of repentance.

The cause of demonic bondage can be significant, but once Jesus had established that the sufferer needed to have a demon cast out, he did not attempt to establish the cause – only to expel the spirit. In fact, the Gospels describe Jesus asking only two questions in the course of his casting out ministry – in Mark 5:9 & Mark 9:21.

But, as we shall see in Part Nine, the Holy Spirit may show you some relevant facts about how the demon entered the person and what might be a reason for the ongoing demonic influence. There are no hard-and-fast rules concerning this, only that we should be ready to listen to the information and direction that the Holy Spirit gives in any specific situation.

3. Jesus spoke directly to the demon
Only in the encounter with the crippled woman does Jesus appear to have conversed at length with the sufferer. In the other instances his authoritative words of ministry were directed at the evil spirit controlling or influencing the person.

Clearly, Jesus did not ignore the sufferer, and his ministry was within the context of offering spiritual support and direction to the person. It is important we recognise, however, that – during the actual time of ministry – Jesus spoke directly to the demon.

We have seen that Jesus came to undo the works of the devil, so when a work of Satan was brought to his attention he got straight on with his messianic task of destroying it. In Jesus' ministry to those afflicted with spirits, the Gospels record five things he said directly to demons.

'Be bound'
Mark 1:25 & Luke 4:35 state that Jesus said 'Be quiet' to the unclean spirit. Mark 1:26, however, reports that the spirit gave a loud cry.

The Greek verb *phimoo* is better translated as 'to muzzle' than 'to silence' – and is translated as that in I Corinthians 9:9 & I Timothy 5:18. It seems that Jesus ordered unclean spirits to be bound or to be restricted, and this involves silence or quiet but is not restricted to that.

In Matthew 12:29, Jesus made it clear that 'the strong man' must first be tied up. This is what he did in the Capernaum synagogue, and this is a preliminary stage to the ejection of the demon.

'Be rebuked'

The use of the verb *epitimao* – to rebuke – is related to binding. *Epitimao* literally means 'to set a weight upon' and is used in relation to demons in Matthew 17:18; Mark 1:25; 9:25; Luke 4:35, 41 & 9:42. It is used in exactly the same way in Luke 4:39 about the fever affecting Peter's mother-in-law. It is the use of *epitimao* here which suggests that this story is more about casting out a demon than healing.

Epitimao was also used by Jesus in Matthew 8:26; Mark 4:39 & Luke 8:24 – suggesting that the wind was a demonic attack. The sentence construction in Mark 4:39 is the same as in Mark 1:25: Jesus rebuked, and then illustrated this by using *phimoo*. 'Be bound' was the expression of his rebuke, the setting of a divine weight upon the spirit.

'Come out'

In the stories of the Capernaum, Gadarene and epileptic demoniacs, Jesus commanded the demons to 'come out.' This simple command was the basic phrase used by Christ in his casting out ministry.

Questions

In Mark 5:9, Jesus asked the demon, 'What is your name?' Mark and Luke both show that Jesus had been commanding the spirit to come out for some while, perhaps even from before the boat had landed on the beach. This is similar to the two-stage healing of the blind man in Mark 8:22–26, and suggests that Jesus' question was more a second stage of attack than a polite enquiry.

In biblical times, a person's name and nature were considered to be indistinguishable – to know someone's name was to know their nature. The demon's ambiguous reply and reaction in 5:9–10 make sense when we realise that Jesus' words were not just a question to establish a handle to aid future ejection, they were also a command for the spirit to expose itself by revealing its nature.

This self-revelation was the demonic signal of defeat. Jesus' words of command – which we can better understand as, 'Show your nature' – had sufficed. He did not need to repeat the command, 'Get out.'

Interestingly, Jesus' other question was also asked after ministry had been going on for some while. In Mark 9:14–29, the disciples could not expel the demon, and the epileptic boy was brought to Jesus. By his question, Jesus could have been trying to expose the nature of the demon, or (because a child was involved) he could have been enquiring about possible hereditary factors.

It is not clear whether Jesus' explanation, in verse 29, suggests that he had recognised a particular kind of spirit or a special kind of demonic oppression. Either way, it was clearly a severe case, and Jesus used an emphatic personal pronoun (which is better rendered as, 'It is I who command you') which deliberately drew attention to himself and his resources.

'Don't return'
Jesus' final words to the evil spirit in Mark 9:25 were 'and never enter him again'. It may simply be that this demon had been working intermittently, as Mark 9:25 suggests; but Jesus does mention the possibility of evil spirits returning to a person after they have been cast out in Matthew 12:43–45 & Luke 11:24–26.

This was a prolonged, persistent, violent and destructive case, and Jesus was dealing with the situation exactly as it was.

The fact that the Gospels do not report Jesus speaking this command in ministry to anyone else illustrates the importance of listening to the Spirit and following his instructions. Jesus did not have a set pattern for ministry which he followed in every situation – and neither should we.

4. Jesus made no distinction between sufferers

Many leaders make much of classifications of demonic suffering and demonic grip. They use a wide variety of words to describe a host of different conditions: for example, 'oppression', 'possession', 'depression', 'infestation', 'influence', 'attack' and 'affliction'.

The Gospels do not suggest that Jesus made much use of such distinctions. One Greek word, *daimonizomai*, is used to describe almost everyone who needed to be released from a demon. Superficially, the people seemed to have different conditions; but, in reality, their problems all had an identical root. *Daimonizomai* describes the root problem, not the surface symptoms.

Daimonizomai is usually translated as 'possessed', which implies control or ownership; but *daimonizomai* really means 'demon afflicted': the transliteration 'demonised' is more helpful – and far less controversial.

This means that the most important questions we can ask the Spirit in deliverance ministry are, 'What ministry does this person need?' and 'Is this person demonised?' The woman in Luke 13 would have appeared to have had a very different problem from the man in Mark 5, but Jesus knew in the Spirit that they both needed a demon cast out.

Again, this underlines just how important it is for us to listen to the Spirit, to ask him questions, and to rely on his direction. There are some cases, as in Mark 5, where it seems obvious that a demon must be cast out – even so, we should still seek his direction and prompting. But there are other cases – as in Luke 13 – where we depend entirely on the Spirit for insight.

5. Jesus distinguished exorcism from healing

The stories about the dumb demoniac and Peter's mother-in-law could, on their own, suggest that the Gospels confuse exorcism with healing. But Matthew 8:16; Mark 1:32–34; Luke 4:40–41; 6:18 & 7:21 show a clear difference between healing the sick and casting out demons. And Matthew 4:24 makes an important distinction between *daimonizomai* and *seleniazomai* – between demonisation needing deliverance and insanity or epilepsy needing healing.

When Jesus helped the crippled woman, he first released her from her bondage to Satan, then laid his hands on her to heal her bent back. It seems to be the same with Peter's mother-in-law: Luke records the initial breaking of Satan's grip, whereas Matthew and Mark record the healing touch which followed.

6. Jesus' source of authority

In Jesus' day, itinerant Jewish exorcists cast out demons using long lists of names and even mechanical aids. Some of them even tried to use Jesus' name – in Mark 9:38 with success, and in Acts 19:13–16 with spectacular failure! Jesus, however, needed to use no authority other than his own.

In Matthew 12:28, he claimed to eject demons through the Spirit of God. (Luke 11:20 uses 'finger of God' – from Exodus 8:19 & Psalm 8:3.) Jesus' ministry was a personal confrontation between the one who was full of the power of the Holy Spirit and an unclean spirit – so Jesus was totally dependent on his anointing with the Spirit.

Mark 9:29 offers another reason for Jesus' effectiveness. As he did not pray between his arrival and the ministry, this must refer to preparatory prayer and fasting. We should note that, as in Jesus' healing ministry, there is an absence of prayer during the time of ministry.

Matthew 17:19–20 adds a third reason – which we consider later – mountain-moving faith.

7. Jesus terrified demons

The Gospels show that demons vary in their evil powers, are intent on people's destruction, bring disease, speak, are enormously strong, possess supernatural knowledge, and that several can influence or afflict a person simultaneously.

The Gospel examples also show that, even before their defeat at Calvary, demons were terrified of Jesus! Instead of remaining silent in his presence, they were so afraid that they shrieked and exposed themselves. They always had to obey Jesus. When he said 'Come out,' they came out – even if their departures were noisy and violent.

8. People reacted to Jesus in different ways

Matthew 12:28 shows that deliverance ministry was at the heart of Jesus' kingdom message. The rightful ruler had come, and the usurper was being put to flight.

After Jesus had cast out demons, Mark 1:21–28 reports astonishment and a spreading reputation; Luke 9:43 comments that the crowds were awe-struck by the greatness of God; and Luke 8:37 describes panic and an urgent request for Jesus to leave the area. Of those released, however, only the man in Mark 5:18 is recorded as begging to follow Jesus.

The most terrible reaction of all is recorded in Luke 11:15; Mark 3:22; Matthew 9:34 & 12:24. Jesus' detractors accused him of being possessed by Beelzebub, of being mad and ministering hand in hand with Satan himself. These accusations were also made in John 7:20; 8:48, 52 & 10:20. We should not, therefore, be surprised when those who serve with Christ in this ministry today face similar hostility.

The disciples cast out demons

Jesus never sent people out to preach the gospel without also giving them his authority to heal sickness and cast out demons. We have seen that Jesus trained about eighty disciples to share in his healing ministry, and Matthew 10:8; 17:19; Luke 9:1 & 10:17 show that they also shared in his ministry of casting out demons.

Luke 10:17–20 is important. The disciples rejoiced, 'Lord, even the demons are subject to us in your name.' The Greek verb *hupotasso* – 'to submit' or 'to be subject' is a military term meaning 'rank under' or to lose or surrender one's own rights or will. The disciples confronted the demons not with their own personal authority – as Jesus did – but with the authority of Jesus. This is a basic principle of all deliverance ministry.

Jesus' reply in Luke 10:18–20 is illuminating. The tense of 'I saw' means 'I have been seeing Satan falling' and suggests that Satan's fall was continuous, rather than an event, and was associated with their casting out ministry. This means that, throughout the mission, at every expulsion of a demon, Jesus saw Satan fall. Jesus' comparison with lightning means that the fall was spectacular and obvious.

The endings of both Matthew's and Mark's Gospels suggest that the ministry of casting out demons was meant to continue in the life of the church. Mark 16:17 lists deliverance ministry as the first of the signs to be associated with believers. The Great Commission, Matthew 28:19–20, instructs the disciples to teach all future disciples to observe all Jesus' commands – and that, presumably, includes Matthew 10:8.

The book of Acts records eight specific incidents of healing, but only one example of a demon being cast out – 16:16–18. There are three general statements about the ministry: 5:12–16; 8:4–8 & 19:11–20. These passages need careful study.

The Philippian slave-girl
The appearance of the slave-girl, Acts 16:16–18, may have, at first, been welcome. Paul had faced misunderstanding and hostility in previous towns, yet here was a girl who knew Paul, Silas and Luke, knew the content of their message, and was ready to act as their herald.

But the three apostles soon realised that she was a fortune-teller. Some translations of Acts 16:16 suggest that the girl was possessed by a 'spirit of divination', but a literal translation of *pneuma puthona* would be 'python-spirit'.

(Python was the name in Greek mythology of the Pythias dragon which dwelt at the foot of Mount Parnassus guarding the oracle of Delphi. It was slain by Apollo and the name was transferred to Apollo and was often applied to soothsayers or fortune-tellers. These were regarded as being inspired by Apollo when they acted as spirit-ventriloquists.)

Paul's words in 16:18 follow those of Jesus. He did not deal with the demon on the basis of his personal authority, but as the earthly representative of Jesus. The use of the Greek verb *paraggello* – 'to order' – reveals that this ministry had been initiated by Christ's command.

The noun, *paraggelia*, is a military term which is used of commands received by a junior officer from his superior, and then passed on to the ranks. Jesus used *paraggello* in Luke 8:29 when he confronted the Gadarene demoniac. This suggests that he cast out demons when his Father instructed him to do so by the Spirit.

This incident, though set in an evangelistic context, reports no conversions. The Philippian crowd were not impressed; we do not know if the girl was converted; and Paul was flogged, thrown in jail and fastened in stocks – the price he had to pay for his share in this element of Jesus' ministry in the Spirit.

Peter's shadow
The ministry described in Acts 5:12–16 appears to be part of the answer to the disciples' Acts 4:24–30 intercession. It seems that the people of Jerusalem already held the disciples in great respect, but that the ministry drew in the crowds from the surrounding countryside.

Some Bible teachers suggest that demons were cast out by Peter's shadow. A straightforward reading of 5:15–16, however, suggests that it was only the sick who positioned themselves to be touched by his shadow.

As in the Gospels, a distinction is made between *astheneis*, 'the sick', and *ochloumenoi*, 'those tormented or crowded by evil spirits'; and only the sick are mentioned in verse 15.

Whatever happened, we must note that those who were delivered had first been brought to the church, and that this was a particular moment when God worked in unusual power, perhaps as a consequence of the believers' behaviour in Acts 4:24–30.

Paul's handkerchiefs and aprons
The Old Testament appears to hint at a belief in the representative power of clothing: for example, Genesis 35:2; Numbers 20:25–26; 1 Samuel 18:3–4; 1 Kings 19:19 & 2 Kings 2:8–14. And Luke 8:43–48 relates the story of the lady who was healed when she touched Jesus' cloak.

Acts 19:11–12 should encourage an open-minded approach and the realisation that God uses people and methods we may disdain. This remarkable ministry took place because God was with Paul in a special way at Ephesus, and because there had been for the evil spirits – even at a distance – a confrontation with Christ in Paul.

Sceva's seven sons
Acts 19:11–16 moves straight from amazing aprons to Sceva's sons. Verse 13 suggests that Paul must have invoked the authority of the name of Jesus in his ministry. Because of Paul's effectiveness, other Jewish preachers tried using the name of the Lord Jesus as a tool in their non-Christian deliverances.

Their spectacular failure demonstrates that casting out demons is not a matter of technique or the recitation of special words. It is an encounter between two forces – one demonic and the other divine.

Sceva's sons fled naked and mauled because their ministry was not the passing on of a command from God, because they were not filled and empowered by the Spirit of God, and because they did not personally know Jesus and had no right to invoke his name.

Repentant believers
Acts 19 then records, in verses 18–20, an incident which is very important to the contemporary ministry of deliverance. 'Casting out' ministry may not be described in this passage, but it clearly

is an example of 'deliverance' ministry. Under the powerful anointing of the Spirit reported in 19:11–17, believers repented, confessed their sins and destroyed any occult books in their possession.

It was not enough for them just to confess and repent of their sins, they also were led by the Spirit to burn publicly magic books worth 50,000 pieces of silver. This voluntary, total destruction meant that the demonic and occult powers lost their hold on the believers.

Acts 19:20 reports the considerable evangelistic impact of all the different aspects of deliverance ministry described in 19:11–19. This reflects Acts 8:4–8, when multitudes of Samaritans welcomed Philip's message because of the miracles, and the first example given is that 'unclean spirits, crying with a loud voice, came out of many'.

Paul's teaching

From the New Testament evidence, it is reasonable to conclude that the ministry of casting out demons was an important feature of early church life; however, it is not mentioned in the lists of ministers or church officials, or in the lists of spiritual gifts.

Paul frequently shows his belief in the existence of evil forces: for example, Romans 8:38–39; 1 Corinthians 5:5; 7:5; 15:24; 2 Corinthians 2:11; 6:15; 11:14–15; 12:7; Ephesians 3:10; 6:12; Colossians 2:8, 15; 1 Thessalonians 2:18; 2 Thessalonians 2:4, 9 & 3:3. But he never mentions a specialist ministry of casting out demons.

Quite possibly, this is because Paul had believers in mind. The gifts and ministers he describes are for the building up and benefit of the church. It would, therefore, have been inappropriate and unnecessary for him to mention casting out demons.

Paul believed that people were either in Christ or in Satan, that they were guided either by the Spirit or by their sinful nature, that Christians had transferred from darkness to light – from Satan to Christ. This is particularly clear in 2 Corinthians 6:16–7:1.

The New Testament evidence seems to suggest that every Spirit-anointed believer could cast out a demon, but only when they received a clear command from Christ. When casting out a demon, their authority was the name of Christ, and their source of power was the Holy Spirit working through them. They generally worked in partnership with other believers, and prepared themselves with prayer, God's faith, and fasting.

It also seems that, in the early church, the ministry of casting out demons was usually expected in an evangelistic context, as Christ's body on earth confronted and embraced those outside God's kingdom who were held in the strong grip of the evil one. We would do well to learn from their example.

Part Nine

The deliverance ministry today

We have seen that Jesus preached liberty to the captives, set the down- trodden free, and destroyed the devil's work. He now continues this ministry through his Church, and the Great Commission indicates that this should reach to all nations and continue until the end of time.

We have also recognised that 'deliverance' is a broad concept. Everybody needs deliverance. All people need once-for-all deliverance from sin, guilt and death; all believers need daily deliverance from faults, blunders and temptations; and some people need deliverance from evil spirits. We should emphasise the first two aspects of deliverance ministry, without ignoring or down-playing the third.

Then there is the larger area of deliverance in society. In *The Rule of God* we examine how the Church is the world's light and salt, and effects changes in the world's thinking, behaviour and structures by its service, sacrifice and prayer. The Church's purpose is worship, but its mission is deliverance. Our eyes should be fixed on Jesus, while our feet stamp heavily on the works of Satan.

Warnings

As part of the ministry of deliverance, we have a responsibility to warn people about those supernatural activities which claim to be of God, but which are not carried out in his name and power.

The word 'occult' is often used to describe these practices, which comes from the Latin word for 'secret' – *occultus*. However, these things are no longer hidden or secretive, so 'occult' is not an accurate word. The practices are supernatural, but they are evil in origin and nature rather than holy.

The Bible expressly prohibits human involvement with evil supernatural practices and shows that God hates and opposes them. It is important we note that the Scriptures state that any involvement with these practices leads to divine punishment. We see this, for example, in Exodus 22:18; Leviticus 19:26, 31; Deuteronomy 18:9–12; 32:16–17; 2 Kings 21; 1 Chronicles 10:13; Psalm 106; Acts 16:16–18; 19:18–19; 1 Corinthians 10:20–22; Revelation 9:21; 21:8 & 22:15.

Evil practices can be divided into three areas.

◆　Miracles

God's reality is any miracle which is worked in the name of Jesus. An evil miracle is any wonder not worked in the power and authority of his holy name; this includes black or white magic (not conjuring tricks), divination, levitation, acts of strength, astral projection and the many forms of so-called spiritual healing.

◆　Communication

God's provision is prayer to the Father, in the Spirit, through the Son. The satanic version of this is any attempt at spirit communication – innocent or deliberate – which is not Christian prayer. This includes ouija, seances, spiritism, spiritualism and so on.

◆　Knowledge of the future

God's revelation can be found in the Bible and through Christian prophecy. Demons communicate through evil practices like palmistry, astrology, tarot, mirror mantic, psychometry, divination and the teaching in demonic text books.

The Bible gives five reasons why these evil practices are forbidden.

◆　Genesis 3 shows that God has placed boundaries on knowledge, and the desire for knowledge not normally available to humanity is the motivating force in many evil practices. As in Eden, the devil traps many in bondage and death through this thirst for knowledge.

◆ A desire to dominate and control people, objects, events and the future is normally either the reason for, or the result of, involvement in evil practices. This desire is the opposite of humanity's right nature and is condemned in Isaiah 47:12–15 & Ezekiel 13:17–23.

◆ Involvement is dangerous and frequently leads to demonic control and to some element of psychological disintegration or physical destruction. There are many scriptural examples – the story of Saul is striking – but a recent example can be more persuasive.

◆ It is an attempt to make contact with forces which are at war with God. As we will see later, this is why the Bible teaches that God punishes believers who turn from following him to being involved with any evil practice.

◆ God has said, 'No!' Such practices are expressly forbidden in the New Testament – though it must be remembered that they are normally mentioned in association with other sins that God finds equally repugnant. Galatians 5:19–21, for example, condemns sorcery alongside jealousy, bad temper and quarrels. It is wrong to suggest that some sins are more sinful than others, and to infer that people are spiritually safe as long as they avoid demonic practices.

Passing on God's thoughts about evil practices is one element of our deliverance ministry, but we confront evil forces more powerfully and persuasively by ministering in the power of God's Holy Spirit.

Prayer
Believers and churches which expect to confront Satan's forces directly need to be thoroughly prepared by persistent, united prayer. In Mark 9:29, Jesus said that prayer was the difference between his disciples' ineffective ministry and his own

effectiveness. If Christ needed preparatory prayer, then so must we. This should include the united prayer of the whole local church. We examine this in Part Seven of *Effective Prayer*.

The ministry described in Acts 5:12–16 was the result of the united prayer reported in Acts 4:24–30. The deliverance of the Philippian slave-girl in Acts 16:16–18 follows on from a description of a riverside prayer meeting in verse 13, and verse 16 shows that this prayer was not an isolated occurrence.

If it is thought that a demon needs to be cast out, the local church should be alerted to intercede for the 'casting out' ministry: this should include prayer for boldness, guidance, wisdom, power and brevity.

Evangelism
In the New Testament, the casting out of demons is usually set in an evangelistic context, but this does not mean that all converts need this ministry. Everybody who turns to Christ should be encouraged, as in 1 Thessalonians 1:9, to break with every form of idolatry so that they can become effective servants of the real and living God.

New converts need to appreciate what practices are incompatible with following Christ, to repent of past involvement and promise future purity. They need to learn about, and claim by faith and baptism, the full freedom of God's forgiveness.

Many converts will have been involved with some forms of demonic practice. Most of these will need, like the Acts 19:18–19 believers, only to confess their sins, renounce their involvement, and destroy any possessions which were part of these demonic practices. There will be some converts, however, who also need to be released from a demon.

Diagnosis
In the Scriptures, the commonest symptoms of *daimonizomai*, 'demonisation', were:

◆   A permanent loss of self-control
◆   Or, a temporary loss of control when confronted by Christ

◆   Or, a severe physical disability.

Any loss of control was demonstrated, for example, by some of these:

◆   Suicidal tendencies

◆   Unusual strength

◆   Violence

◆   A vocal outburst involving supernatural knowledge

◆   A complete change in voice.

Although at least one of these symptoms of 'demonisation' existed in most of the New Testament examples, we urgently need the Spirit's insight in every instance: we need him to reveal to us when a person is 'demonised' and what we should do.

In the Bible, most people with severe physical disabilities, mental illness or epilepsy, did not need to have a demon cast out. But some did, and we will only know who needs deliverance by listening to the Holy Spirit, and by testing what we understand him to be suggesting by the Scriptures and the spiritual gift of *diakrisis*.

As servants of Christ and fellow-servants with him, we are called to destroy the works of Satan. This means that we should be ready to minister deliverance whenever God shows us that a demon is present, and whenever a demon reacts to Christ 'in us' by causing the sufferer to lose self-control and exhibit some of the biblical symptoms.

In many cases, as in the New Testament examples, it is obvious when somebody needs this help, and then there should be no hesitation. We need to ask God only two simple questions. 'Who should be my partner in ministry?' and, 'What exactly, should we say and do?'

At other times, we will need the Spirit's insight – especially when identifying anyone with a severe disability as 'demonised'. In such cases, the Spirit often gives a growing conviction or prophetic 'burden' that deliverance ministry is the appropriate help. This should be shared with the leaders in the local church, and guidance should be sought from God as to when and how such ministry should be given.

Medical help
We should not overlook the fact that a doctor was present at the only detailed example of 'casting out' ministry in Acts, and must recognise that professional medical help benefits many people today.

It is a mistake, however, to think that deliverance ministry is appropriate only for people who remain unhelped after a lengthy programme of medical treatment.

In a modern situation like Mark 1:21–26, it would be crazy to ask the man to sit down and wait while we arranged for him to see a psychiatrist. But it would be equally ridiculous not to refer a sufferer to a doctor if they remained unchanged after several sessions of ministry.

'Casting out' ministry

The following are simple guidelines to help believers faced with a demon to be cast out. They are suggestions to be considered, not rules to be obeyed.

Do not be dictated to by circumstances or people
Our calling is to obey God, to do his will, and not to be pressurised by people. Obedience to the Spirit's prompting sometimes means not helping a sufferer and appearing to be rather heartless; at other times it means instant action. In every situation we should be available to God, yet not presumptuous – ensuring that we ask the Spirit whether he wants to use us, or nobody, or a different believer.

Do not be fearful
In the face of a violent loss of self-control there will always be some apprehension and distress. Our approach should be the same as to death and dying. The Christian is not afraid of death, whereas the process of dying can be very unpleasant. We have

no need to fear the demon – the promise of Luke 10:19 is absolute – but the demonic reaction to Christ can be distressing.

If we are fearful, we should ask Christ to remove our fears and fill us with his self-confidence. Passages like Psalms 124 & 125 are helpful.

Be well prepared
We should ensure that our total dependence is upon Christ and not on any technique, form of words or pattern of ministry; and that we have no bitterness, broken relationship or sin which has not been dealt with.

We should check that we have prayed, fasted, and asked for the Spirit's help; that we have a ministry partner and the prayerful support of our local church; and that we have deep compassion, patience and love for the sufferer. We need to do everything necessary to prevent interruptions, and to remind ourselves that confession, repentance and receiving God's forgiveness may be all that is needed.

Prepare the sufferer
If the person is in control of themselves, we should help them to relax and explain what will happen at each stage of the ministry. We should point out that we will be speaking to the demon during the ministry and not to them, and that their release will be accomplished by Christ alone.

Most sufferers long to be free, and they can be urged to resist the devil themselves, to claim God's promises of freedom, and to add their 'Amen' to the authoritative commands. They can also be encouraged to resist the temptation to surrender to any unnecessary responses – such as shouting and extreme or repetitious bodily movements.

It is often helpful to get the sufferer to read aloud a relevant New Testament story or re-assuring scriptural passage.

Confession and renunciation
Sufferers sometimes lose control to the demon during the time of preparation; for example, during prayer, when the Bible is

read, or when we refer to the cross or the name of Jesus. If this happens it is usually wise to move straight into authoritative commands.

If there is no loss of self-control, the sufferer should be encouraged to confess the sins which the Holy Spirit brings to mind and embrace the power and freedom of God's forgiveness. Acts 19:18 stresses that the believers' confessions of their demonic practices were 'in detail'. Those ministering should announce God's forgiveness, and effectively counsel the person into a realisation of their forgiveness.

If possible at this time, any books, objects or clothes which relate to the demonic practices confessed and forgiven should be destroyed. If this is not possible, the intention should be established of destroying them at the first opportunity.

At this point the people ministering should be alert to anything the Holy Spirit may be revealing about the circumstances of the person's condition. It may be a specific sin that has been committed or a specific traumatic event or even particular contact with the demonic realm through occult activity. Sometimes this information is crucial for the person's freedom and release.

Authoritative commands

If a demon reacts to Christ's presence, or it is plain that a demon needs to be cast out, a few authoritative orders should be spoken. These commands are made on behalf of Jesus: we must be clear that it is only he who casts out demons – those ministering are merely his representatives. This means that special gestures, words, places, dress and objects have no value. It is through his earthly body that Christ confronts the evil force, and we can do no more, and need do no more, than stand there and speak God's commands 'in the name of Jesus'.

Some leaders make much of using the Lord's Prayer or the Lord's Supper when casting out demons. Others think that the Holy Spirit needs a special invitation. Still more people symbolically sprinkle blood around, while many insist that only a special few should minister. No special techniques, however, are taught in Scripture.

Due to mistakes in the past, some churches have felt it is wise to make certain regulations about the ministry of casting out demons, and these should, of course, be respected. But any believer who is in Christ and is anointed with the Holy Spirit can effectively announce commands to expel a demon.

These are only simple guidelines for 'casting out' ministry; the most important matter is to listen to, and to obey, the Holy Spirit.

The demon can be bound or rebuked with words like these:

'I bind you, every evil spirit, in the name of Jesus Christ our Lord and by the power of the Holy Spirit. I command you to be silent and still.'

Demons often try to bring disruption or confusion, a mental blankness or sense of drowsiness. The 'binding' prevents this from happening, or stops it when it has already begun. It also prevents the demon from hurting the sufferer and affecting the ministers.

The demon can be ordered to leave by saying something like this:

'I command you, every evil spirit, in the name of Jesus Christ our Lord and by the power of the Holy Spirit, to go from this person whom you hold captive.'

It may be necessary, as with Jesus and the Gadarene demoniac, to repeat these commands several times.

If the person is still not in control of himself, it may be helpful to read some relevant verses, claim God's promises afresh, cry out to Jesus to deliver the sufferer, and pray in tongues for a short while before repeating the two simple commands.

If there is still no improvement after that, it may be right to order the demon to surrender by revealing its nature. Often, this is the point at which those ministering need to pay careful attention to what the Spirit is revealing about the person's condition. Sometimes, deliverance is delayed until underlying issues are exposed and resolved. There may a need for a deeper repentance, renunciation of demonic contacts or the granting of forgiveness to those who have sinned against the person being ministered to.

Once any such issues have been dealt with it may be necessary to repeat the deliverance commands, identifying the character of the demon. We can say, for example, something like:

> *'In the name of Jesus Christ and by the power of the Holy Spirit, I command you, evil spirit which causes this person to injure himself, to go from them.'*

Some leaders suggest that we should always order demons not to return, and others always command the evil spirit to go to hell or the lake of fire. If it is felt necessary to direct the demon in some way, it is probably best to say something like this:

> *'I hand you over to Jesus Christ for him to deal with as he sees fit.'*

After-care

Jesus' words in Luke 8:39 are the only after-care mentioned in the New Testament in relation to deliverance ministry. We do well to repeat them. The possibility mentioned in Luke 11:24–26, however, suggests that sufferers should be given some good advice.

It appears sensible that the people we serve should be encouraged to turn to Christ, and to believe, be baptised and receive the Holy Spirit. They should be warned about the certainty of counter-attacks by Satan, especially along the lines of old weaknesses, and taught how to resist temptation and claim God's protection.

Once again, we see the relevance of the cell ministry. Discipleship is absolutely necessary for every believer, but especially for those who are receiving ministry for release from demonic activity. Not only do the cells give the opportunity for ongoing discipleship, but they also provide much-needed pastoral care and friendship.

When ministry seems to be ineffective
Sometimes we fare no better than the disciples in Luke 9:40. We must not be embarrassed to acknowledge when nothing has happened, nor must we neglect to spend time asking God why we have been ineffective.

It may be that the sufferer needs directing to a medical practitioner; or that the demon was not confronted by Christ in our life, and we ourselves need cleansing from sin before the person can be delivered.

Whatever the reason, we must go on loving the sufferer, caring for them and praying for their deliverance.

Casting a demon from a believer
Many people ask whether a Christian can be 'possessed'. We have already seen that the word 'possessed' is an inaccurate translation of *daimonizomai*. The word 'possession' suggests the ideas of control and ownership whereas *daimonizomai* means 'demon afflicted'.

Obviously someone who belongs to Christ cannot be under the control of the devil. Areas of our lives, however, can come under demonic influence – but only if we allow this to happen. In some cases, it may be necessary for believers to receive deliverance ministry which involves casting out a demon.

Although deliverance ministry may occasionally be necessary to help some believers become fully free from some sinful practices, 'casting out' ministry is no solution to ordinary sinful habits and fleshly self-indulgence. Romans 8:12–13 & Ephesians 4:17–32 show that these things cannot be 'cast out'; they have to be 'put off', 'put to death', 'crucified'.

But a demon may need to be cast out if there is an unnatural – a spiritual or a supernatural – dimension to the particular sinful habit or condition, and the 'normal' Christian disciplines of sanctification have proved to be insufficient to bring freedom.

Some leaders argue that such deliverance ministry is always unnecessary and unbiblical. They maintain that believers are in Christ and in the Spirit, so there cannot be a need for a demon to be cast out.

Ephesians 2:1–3 describes what we were like before we believed in Jesus. We were dead to God and alive to the world, the flesh and the devil. But now we are alive to God and dead to the world, the flesh and the devil. We are seated with Christ in the heavenlies – we are delivered.

But our *legal position* in Christ does not automatically describe our *present experience* in Christ. There are many things about all our lives which do not agree with our heavenly position, and experiential freedom from demonic affliction must be claimed along with every other blessing which is ours by right in Christ.

If a believer does not appropriate this freedom – or if they allow Satan to gain some influence over their life through sin, indifference or disobedience – the possibility must exist that a demon could achieve a level of affliction which means it needs to be cast from the believer.

Acts 19:10–20; I Corinthians 10:14–22; 12:1–3; Galatians 4:9; 5:19–21; Ephesians 4:26–27; Colossians 2:8; I Timothy 4:1; 2 Timothy 2:25–26 & I Peter 5:8 all suggest that areas of believers' lives may come under varying degrees of demonic affliction.

We must maintain, however, that no demon, not even Satan himself, can ever have total, absolute or final control over the life of any Christian believer.

Protection
Luke 10:19 is a precious promise, but it has meaning only if evil beings exist whose aim is to hurt those who are committed to mission.

Psalms 91; 124 & 125 teach that God really does keep us safe, but it is safety within attack, not immunity from attack. Ephesians 6:17 mentions God's provision of a helmet of safety; but we should appreciate that helmets reduce the effects of a blow – they do not eliminate the possibility of blows. We consider this more fully in Part Seven of *Effective Prayer*.

Finally, we must grasp that the ministry of deliverance does not depend on what we know about demons, but on whether Christ knows us. It depends on weak, fallible believers who know that their Christ has fought and won the decisive battle over Satan; who know that, in union with Christ, they can share in that victory; and who are ready at all times to minister in the power of the Holy Spirit to the hurting people around them.

Part Ten

Speaking with prophetic authority

After healing and deliverance, a third way that Jesus serves particular men and women, and teaches his disciples to serve in the Spirit, is by speaking with his prophetic authority to announce either God's blessing or his judgement.

What is God's blessing?
The Hebrew verb for bless is *barak*, and its companion noun is *berakah*. Their basic meaning is 'someone kneeling to give prosperity'. The New Testament equivalent is *eulogeo* which means 'to speak well of a person'.

Ahere and *makarios*, the Hebrew and Greek words for 'happy', are translated as 'blessed' in some Bibles, but they describe a result of blessing rather than the act of blessing itself.

We can define God's blessing as 'words spoken in the authority of God's name which bring a tangible, physical, material or spiritual benefit to an individual, family, nation or church – and which may continue from generation to generation'.

God's blessing

Exodus 20:4–6 introduces a jealous God who punishes to the third and fourth generations, but who also shows kindness to those who love him – to the thousandth generation.

Deuteronomy 7:7–15 expands on this. God's judgement or cursing is limited, but his blessing is unlimited. He is faithful and true. His blessing is constant. Deuteronomy 5:8–10; Nehemiah 9:17–37; Psalm 86:15 & James 1:17–18 reveal the character of our God who blesses.

God's first blessing was spoken to the fish and the birds in Genesis 1:21–22. This suggests that the essence of God's blessing is fruitfulness and multiplication – physical reproduction with many children, and spiritual reproduction to fill the earth with God's children.

God blessed humanity this way in Genesis 1:28; 5:2 & 9:1. This aspect of God's blessing runs through Scripture and continues today. Is my local church blessed? Is it fruitful and multiplying? It is the same question. According to the Scriptures, we are either blessed in our multiplication or judged in our barrenness.

The story of Abraham teaches much about God's blessing. Genesis 11:27–12:9 could imply that the blessing might have been Terah's; but he settled down in Haran, and the seven-fold blessing of Genesis 12:1–3 was announced to his seventy-five year old son. Twenty-five years later, in 17:15–22, the blessing spread to Sarah, and Abraham asked for it to extend to Ishmael as well.

God granted Ishmael the physical blessings of fertility, fruitfulness and multiplication, but he would not bless him spiritually. In the Old Testament, God's physical blessings were freely given, but his spiritual blessings were restricted to those whom he chose.

Deuteronomy 8:13–15 & 28:1–14 list fertility, health, victory, prosperity, good reputation, family harmony and success as classic Old Testament evidences of God's blessing. Common grace means that these extended to unbelievers, but they were also special divine rewards for obedience to the Law.

We know that, in Christ, the door has been opened for us to experience an infinite degree of blessing. But God chooses which particular physical blessings he gives to any person or family. The level of our blessing may be determined by the degree of our obedience, but the type of our *physical* blessing is determined only by the will of God.

Spiritual blessings, however are freely available in Christ. Ephesians 1:4–14 shows that spiritual blessings are brought or activated by the Spirit, and it lists election, holiness, living in

God's presence, adoption, the gift of grace, freedom through forgiveness, revelation and salvation. Verses 13–14 reveal the Holy Spirit himself as the present pledge of our eternal heritage of divine blessing.

It seems that God tests those he chooses to bless, but only so that he can increase their blessing. Genesis 22 demonstrates the faith of both Abraham and Isaac. Because of their obedient faith, in verses 16–18, God showered blessings on Abraham; and, in 25:11, on Isaac.

Jacob also wanted God's blessing but – because he went about it the wrong way – God did not voluntarily bless Jacob. Only when Jacob had been humbled, and had begged for divine blessing, did God respond in 32:29: this is quoted in 48:4 and fulfilled in Exodus 1:7. In Genesis 39:2–6 & 41:52, the spiritual blessing passed to Joseph, and then to the nation of Israel. Deuteronomy 7:7–16 explains why the Jews were chosen for this special blessing.

Finally, the divine blessing was extended from the believing children of Israel to embrace the Church of God. (We consider this in Part Six of *Glory in the Church*.)

Conditions for divine blessing
The Bible gives three conditions for God to bless a person or group.

1. We must be in the place which God has chosen to bless
2 Samuel 6:9–11 illustrates this. Obed-Edom was blessed by God simply because he lived where the ark of Yahweh was dumped. 1 Chronicles 26:1–8 reveals the extent of his blessing!

God's Old Testament spiritual blessings were restricted to those in the covenant relationship, and his New Testament blessing is restricted to those who are in the New Covenant, to believers in Christ. God's blessing is not available to those people who are not living in the right place – to those who are not in the Spirit, in Christ Jesus.

2. Faith-inspired obedience which is rooted in love
Deuteronomy 7:7–11; 28:1–14; 30:15–20 & John 14–16
make this clear. John 14–16 interweaves love, obedience and
blessing, all culminating in the spiritual blessing of the promise
of the gift of the Holy Spirit.

3. A right treatment of the poor
Deuteronomy 15:4–18 establishes the link, and Deuteronomy
23:19–20 & 24:14–22 expand the principle. It is not only
wrong to be apathetic towards the poor, the despised, widows,
orphans and strangers: it is foolishly counter-productive.

This is hinted at in Psalm 41:1–2; Proverbs 11:24–26; Isaiah
58:6–12; Luke 12:33 & 1 Timothy 6:18–19. It is explicitly
stated in Proverbs 22:9; 2 Corinthians 9:6–15 & Matthew
25:31–46; and is seen in action in Acts 2:45–47 & 6:1–7.

God's judging

The Bible reveals that the living God delights to bless to the
thousandth generation, but that he will judge or 'curse' to the
third generation when there is a just cause. In the Old
Testament, God's judgements upon people and nations were
commonly called 'curses'.

Genesis 3:14–15, 16 & 17–19 record God's first three
judgements or curses, and show that God does not judge
without reason. The serpent was cursed because he had
tempted Eve. The woman was cursed because she had
disobeyed God. And Adam was cursed because he had
listened to his wife and eaten from the forbidden tree.

The curse on the serpent opposes the human race to the
devil, hints at God's ultimate victory, and provides the first glimpse
of salvation. The curses on Adam and Eve are appropriate to their
functions: the woman suffers as mother and wife, the man as
bread-earner. Death is added to these punishments in verse 19,
and the loss of intimacy with God in verse 23.

These first curses are permanent and hereditary. Romans 5
compares our solidarity in Christ as Saviour with our solidarity

in Adam as sinner. All humanity is still affected by these curses today, and they will cease to operate only when the day of Revelation 22:3 dawns.

All God's other judgements or curses directly relate to particular individuals, nations and families, and the Old Testament identifies several key reasons why God curses them.

Anti-Semitism

Genesis 12:1–3 identifies anti-Semitism as a key cause. Through history, many nations which have opposed the different people groups descended from Abraham have, ultimately, been unsuccessful despite their apparent military superiority and initial success.

Genesis 12:3 uses two of the three basic Hebrew words for the verb 'to curse'. God will *arar* those who *qalal* Abraham.

◆ *Arar* means to curse thoroughly in a premeditated manner with the intention of bringing about great harm. It appears fifty-four times in the Old Testament and is normally used only to describe a judgement or curse by God.

◆ *Qalal* means to revile or vilify in a casual way, to esteem lightly, to make a contemptuous comment, to slight.

◆ *Qabab* is the third Hebrew verb for 'to curse' which is used in the Old Testament. It means to pierce, to bore through with a hole, to execrate, to stab someone with words.

Its transliteration *kebab* has come to be the word for the common demonic practice of sticking a pin into the effigy of a person to hurt them by an accident, illness, disaster, or even death.

In the Old Testament, a *qabab* curse is weaker than an *arar* curse, but stronger than *qalal*.

False religions

Deuteronomy 27:15–26 reveals several reasons why God judged his people in the Old Testament. The first, in verse 15, was turning away from worshipping God to follow false gods, or to being involved in false religions or evil practices.

This did not mean that God broke his covenant relationship with those he cursed. Instead, they lost some of their heavenly rewards and stopped enjoying some of God's blessings on earth: to a limited extent, their earthly lives became miserable and difficult.

Other reasons

Other actions which Deuteronomy 27 reveal as causing God to curse his people include to *qalal* one's mother or father. Exodus 21:17; Leviticus 20:9 & Proverbs 20:20 show the seriousness of this: Jesus quoted these passages in Mark 15:4 & 7:10.

Mistreating neighbours, having a wrong attitude to the helpless, committing bestiality, incest or murder, involvement with evil or occult practices – all of these actions put God's Old Testament children under God's *arar*.

Disobedience

Deuteronomy 27:26 reveals the fundamental cause of God's judgement on Israel. Their blessing and cursing pivoted upon their obedience. They either obeyed God and were blessed, or they disobeyed him and were cursed. 2 Chronicles 34:22–28; Jeremiah 11:1–12; 17:5–8 & 29:16–23 point to disobedience as the principle reason for God's curse.

Jeremiah 48:10 shows that God also judged those who did his work half-heartedly.

Greed

Joshua 6:18; Malachi 3:6–12 & 2 Peter 2:14 show that greed, or covetousness, is another important cause of divine judgement. 2 Peter 2 lists the characteristics of false teachers which are hated by God, and verse 14 suggests that greed is near the top of the list.

The usual Greek word for curse, *katara*, is used here. The Old Testament distinctions between different types of curses were not continued, so there is only one New Testament word. This coincides with *arar* – the strongest type of Old Testament curse.

Misusing God's name
Jeremiah 29:23; Zechariah 5:1–4 & Malachi 2:1–9 show that misusing the holy name was the final Old Testament reason for God judging his people. This could be either swearing falsely in his name, or presuming to speak in God's name without a direct order from him.

The Deuteronomy curses today
Many leaders suggest that these Deuteronomy 27 curses still apply to believers today, and that God judges us in a similar way to the people of Israel whenever we break the Mosaic law.

We have seen, however, in Part Five of *The Rule of God* that Jesus' fulfilment of the Law resulted in a change of era. The governing principle of the Christian life is not domination by the Jewish Law; it is a living relationship with Jesus. Matthew 28:18–20 shows that we are to live by his words, not by the requirements of the Old Testament law.

This is graphically underlined by Galatians 2:11–3:29, which makes it transparently clear that Gentile believers are not called to live by the Law. The liberating truth of Galatians 3:13 is that 'Christ has redeemed us from the curse of the Law... so that the blessing of Abraham might come upon the Gentiles in Christ Jesus'.

Wonderfully, this means that none of the Deuteronomy curses apply to us, but that all the blessings are wide open to us. This does not mean that God never judges us when we sin. I Corinthians 11:28–32 shows that many of those who are 'in Christ' have become weak and ill, some have even died, as a punishment from the Lord, and the judgement of Ananias in Acts 5 is most severe.

Rather it means that, in his grace, God does not curse us whenever we break the Law. Instead he chastens us when we fall into habitual sin – this is his holy way of gently encouraging us to return to him.

When God does judge us because of our sin, we still go to heaven when we die. Like Ananias, we might arrive in heaven slightly earlier than anticipated, we might lose some of our heavenly rewards, we might have a miserable time on earth – but our covenant relationship remains unbroken. We remain the eternal children of God.

Blessing by Believers

In the Scriptures, we are called both to bless the name of God and to bless other people in the name of God. The Psalms are full of exhortations to bless God and they give much practical advice on how to go about this.

Psalms 16; 66; 68; 103; 135 & 145 make a good starting point for such a study. Here, however, we are concerned with the blessings that we can receive from God and can minister in the Spirit to others – rather than with the way that we can bless God.

We bless others by prophetically announcing God's blessing. In Jesus' name and authority, in the power of the Spirit, at the prompting of the Spirit, we pass on God's blessing: our anointed, authoritative, prophetic words bring about a tangible, physical, material or spiritual benefit to the person or people we bless.

Matthew 12:36–37 shows that our words really matter: we can minister limitation, unbelief and barrenness by what we say, and so too we can minister growth, faith and fruit by our words of blessing.

The Bible is full of examples of people blessing people. It appears that each of them expected a tangible result from their blessing – they would have been both astonished at any suggestion that they were mouthing empty words or exchanging symbolic greetings.

- Noah blessing Shem and Japheth – Genesis 9:26–27.
- Melchizedek blessing Abraham – Genesis 14:19–20.
- Rebekah being blessed by her mother and brother – Genesis 24:60.
- Jacob blessing Pharaoh – Genesis 47:10.
- Moses blessing the Israelites – Exodus 39:43.
- Joshua blessing Caleb – Joshua 14:13.
- Eli blessing Elkanah and Hannah – 1 Samuel 2:20–21.
- David blessing Barzillai – 2 Samuel 19:39.
- The people blessing the volunteers – Nehemiah 11:2.
- Simeon blessing Mary and Joseph – Luke 2:34.
- Jesus blessing the small children – Mark 10:16.
- Jesus blessing his disciples – Luke 24:50.

Psalm 115:14–15 mentions the blessing of fertility, and this was used in 1 Samuel 2:20–21 & Genesis 24:60. Interestingly, Rebekah then had twins who both went on to found great nations. When we announce a blessing we should expect similar, direct, practical results.

In Luke 10:5–6, Jesus instructed the disciples to bless the members of every house that they entered on their mission. This was not a spoken wish; it was a spiritual gift which was either received or rejected. In John 14:27, Jesus blessed the disciples with the same blessing:

To speak 'Peace' to a family, in the power of the Spirit, is not to mouth an empty formality; rather, it is to minister the coming of the salvation of God with all its associated benefits of wholeness, prosperity, and harmony. If fruitfulness is the essence of God's blessing to men, peace is the primary blessing that we minister to each other.

The Aaronic blessing

Numbers 6:22–27 is a critical passage about the ministry of blessing, and records the form of blessing which God gave to the Aaronic priests. They used it every day in the Temple of Jerusalem when they discharged their priestly responsibility of blessing the children of Israel.

Christ came, died, rose again, ascended and baptised the Church in the Holy Spirit to usher in a new nation of royal priests. This blessing, once restricted to the lips of those in the line of Aaron, can now be used for ever by all in the line of the high priest of the order of Melchizedek. As Hebrews 9:11 makes clear, Jesus Christ was the High Priest of all the blessings.

The Numbers 6 blessing shows us that blessing is an announcement not a prayer. When we bless, we are not asking God to do something; instead, we are ministering God's blessing directly into the life of a person or family. This means that we can bless effectively only those whom he blesses. Our words of blessing are enforced by God only if they have been initiated by the Spirit.

The Aaronic blessing contributes to our understanding of the trinity. The name of God, *Yahweh*, is repeated three times and the blessing is divided into three distinctive sub-blessings which can each be identified with a different member of the Godhead:

- ◆ *Yahweh* bless you and keep you
- ◆ *Yahweh* make his face shine upon you and be gracious to you
- ◆ *Yahweh* lift up his countenance upon you and give you peace.

The first phrase brings the Father's protection down upon the person being blessed. Verse 27 explains the important principle that the ministering of a blessing is the calling down of the name of God upon the person being blessed.

A biblical name is not a mere label, it denotes the real personality and characteristics of the person. In the Bible, to put a name on a person means to place the individual concerned under the influence and protection of the owner of that name.

A major scriptural theme is that protection is the primary function of God's name, that the person who has God's name placed upon them is kept safe by God. We see this, for example, in 1 Kings 8:29; Psalm 20; 44:5; 124; Proverbs 18:10 & John 17:11–12.

The second phrase can be identified with the Son. It is Jesus who has caused the Father to turn and smile at us; it is he who has brought us grace and favour from God. A smiling face is always a sign of pleasure and approval, and this part of the blessing brings a glance from God which indicates his pardon.

The third phrase can be identified with the Holy Spirit, for it is he who brings peace and the permanent indwelling presence of God. It is in the Spirit that God permanently uncovers his face to us.

In blessing, we announce God's *shalom* – his peace of health, rest, security, success and prosperity. This is the same peace which Jesus commanded his disciples to announce.

Laying hands
There appears to be a biblical link between placing, or laying, hands upon the head of a person and blessing them. In Genesis 48:13–20, for example, Jacob laid his hands on his grandchildren's heads when blessing them, and Jesus did the same in Matthew 19:13.

When it was impossible to lay hands on each person, the biblical practice appears to have been to raise both hands towards the people. We see this, for example, in Leviticus 9:22 & Luke 24:50–51.

Jesus' blessing of the disciples at his ascension is amplified in Acts 1:8–9. It appears that his blessing, with hands raised, was partly a commission for particular service. This is rather like Moses' blessing and commissioning of Joshua in Numbers 27:22–23, and the people of Israel's blessing and commissioning of the Levites in Numbers 8:10–17. The seven deacons were blessed and commissioned the same way in Acts 6:6, as were Saul and Barnabas in Acts 13:3.

All these 'blessings and commissionings' were in conjunction with the laying on of hands and were for 'particular active service' rather than for ordination into an office or position. This association between commissioning and blessing is only to be expected. Any person who has been given a difficult task to perform by God surely needs the help of the blessings of peace, safety, spiritual fertility, wholeness, prosperity, and so on.

1 Timothy 4:14 & 2 Timothy 1:6 record that Timothy's blessing and commissioning for service involved the laying on of hands – and both verses refer to a gift of the Spirit being given at the same time.

As all blessing is a foreshadowing of the blessing of the Holy Spirit, it should be expected that there will be an association between blessing, laying on of hands and the gift and gifts of God's Holy Spirit. We see this in Acts 8:17–18 & 19:6.

It seems that three elements are involved when we minister blessing.

1. A person to God dedication
Laying hands on an individual – or raising hands over a crowd – represents a dedication of the person or people to God. It is a giving of the person to the God who guides, protects, equips and strengthens.

Dedication by placing on hands is seen in Numbers 8:16; Exodus 29:10; Leviticus 1:4; 4:15; 16:21 & Numbers 8:12. In these passages, hands were laid on the animal to dedicate it to its useful, brief service as a sacrifice. When we lay hands on people in blessing, we dedicate them to God in the same way – for a specific task, as a living sacrifice.

2. A God to person blessing
The second element is an announcement of God's blessing upon the person. We can bless only those whom God blesses.

If we are certain that the person meets the three conditions of divine blessing, and we are sure that the Holy Spirit is suggesting that he is about to bless the person, a prophetic announcement should be made – for example, 'The peace of the Lord be with you.'

When we are not sure whether the person does meet the divine conditions for blessing, it is better to petition for blessing with words like, 'May the peace of the Lord be with you.'

3. A person to person transference

When hands were laid on the animals to dedicate them for sacrificial service, the sins of the people were symbolically transferred to the animals. Something parallel appears to happen in blessing. It seems that we can normally bless only with a particular blessing that we have ourselves received.

A careful reading of the Old Testament passages suggests that Old Testament believers usually blessed so that the person received something that they themselves had already experienced, if only in part. They therefore expected to be depleted in some way as a result.

In the New Testament, those who had received God's peace were those who ministered it; those who had received the blessing of the Holy Spirit were those who helped others to receive it, and so on.

Blessing today

The ministry of announcing God's blessing can take place at most services. An opportunity can be given for those with a special need for peace, wholeness, prosperity, fertility and so on, to be blessed.

For example:

- ◆ Either the leaders, or those who have experienced the particular aspect of divine blessing which is being sought, should lay hands on the person and give them into God's hands.

◆ They should call on the revealed name of God which is appropriate to the particular need – for example, 'the God of all peace', 'the God who guides', 'the God who protects' and so on, and bless them.

◆ Believers who will be engaging in particular work for God during the week can be commissioned and blessed for their task.

◆ Students returning to college, women advising neighbours, people with non-Christian friends coming for a meal, the man going to pray for a sick friend, all of these can have hands laid on them to dedicate them for their service and to receive the help from the Holy Spirit which they need for their task.

At the very least, this means that their service is seen as the local church at work rather than individuals operating independently. At the best, they are far better equipped for effective service.

Some churches have introduced the ministry of blessing without realising it. They invite people forward to receive 'ministry', and by this they mean that they lay hands on the head of the person and pray over them a prayer relevant to their need. This is almost the ministry of blessing. The difference is that – rather than offering a quick prayer of petition – we listen carefully to the Spirit, test his promptings, and speak his prophetic announcement.

Of course, the ministry of blessing should not be restricted to Christian meetings. Nearly all of the biblical material deals with blessing in private conversation and personal ministry, and we need to develop experience and expertise in this.

We must pray for God's wisdom and direction before we bless. We should always be specific in our blessing, invest it with faith, lay hands, call down the name of God, and – most important of all – speak only the words that the Spirit gives to us.

As with all the different aspects of ministry we have considered, if our words are not 'in the Spirit' they are bound to be barren.

Demonic cursing

The Old Testament makes it plain that 'cursing' can be an evil practice which is enforced by Satan. Certainly, Job 3:8 implies that curses can arouse *Leviathan*. (This refers to a sea-monster which was often used as a poetic description of Satan, for example, Isaiah 27:1.)

Cursing is the opposite of blessing, and we can say that a curse is 'harsh, negative or destructive words spoken against another person, or oneself, with a desire to bring about harm or pain to the person'.

At the most basic human level, we know that idle words of gossip can have unforeseen consequences, and can injure people's lives. There is, however, an evil destroyer who delights to enforce these words and bring about much more severe and wide-ranging results.

Curses against oneself
It is possible to curse oneself, and for this to be enforced by Satan. In Genesis 27, Rebekah pressed Jacob to earn Isaac's blessing by deceit. When Jacob protested that this would leave him vulnerable to a curse, Rebekah spoke the awful words of verse 13. The curse took immediate effect: Jacob had to leave home and Rebekah never saw her son again.

Many people today cursed their bodies when they were young; then, in later life, they wonder what has caused a certain physical problem. The curse must usually be dealt with before healing can begin.

In Matthew 27:24–26, the crowd cursed themselves and their children. This, perhaps, is one reason why Jews down through the ages have found it so hard to believe in Jesus. When they do turn to him, however, they are immediately released from all the effects of the curse.

Curses against subordinates
A curse by someone in a position of authority may also be
enforced by the evil one. In Genesis 31:32 Jacob cursed his
wife – within a short space of time Rachel died in childbirth. In
John 19:15–17, the priests placed their people under a curse,
and, for centuries, the Jews really were ruled by a succession
of other 'Caesars'.

Husbands can curse their wives, parents their children,
employers their employees. A father cries, for example, 'You
are useless' – and the child becomes more useless. A teacher
shouts, 'You will never be as good as your brother,' and a
floundering pupil drops further behind.

These curses are made effective by the authority of the
speaker, and, at times, are enforced by an aroused destroyer.
Very occasionally, God honours the judgmental words of
someone in a position of authority – but only when there is a
just cause and God is himself judging the person. The story of
Jotham's curse in Judges 9:1–57 is an example of this.
Normally, however, these are evil, Satan-honoured curses.

The Bible contains few examples of Satan's servants cursing,
yet hints at a backdrop of cursing. In Numbers 22:1–24:25, for
example, the people of Moab could not defeat Israel in their
own strength, so they turned to Balaam for help and paid him
to curse Israel. Three times, the king of Moab tried to persuade
Balaam to curse the Jews, and each time Balaam blessed them:
he could only curse those whom God was cursing. (This is an
interesting use of the different Hebrew words for curse.
Balaam could only *qabab* – pierce – those whom God *arar* –
had thoroughly cursed.)

It is now a common practice for large companies to call in
demonic help, and, at times, the police do the same:
astrologers, spiritists and clairvoyants are sometimes
summoned to help with their enquiries.

The Church is at war, and curses are in the enemy's
armoury. In 1 Samuel 17:43, Goliath began the battle by

cursing David, and the spiritual army of evil does the same today. David knew how to deal with the curse. Sadly, many modern believers do not.

Announcing God's judgement

In the Scriptures, Judges 5:23 is the only verse which calls on a prophet 'to curse' someone, but the prophets were often inspired to announce God's judgement over a person or nation. We see this expression of national judgement throughout the prophetic books, for example, Amos 1; Nahum & Obadiah. And we see personal words of prophetic judgement in passages like 2 Kings 2:23–25 & Acts 5:7–11.

Peter's words to Sapphira are a clear example of the Numbers 23:8 principle: our words of judgement will be completely useless unless God himself is judging the person.

In Acts 5:1–6, Peter did not judge Ananias. God judged Ananias because he had lied in the name of God and had denied God gifts which had been promised to him. However, when Peter saw that God's judgement was upon the husband, he realised that he had the spiritual authority to announce the same judgement to Ananias' wife – if she met the same conditions.

Paul's prophetic judging

The New Testament describes two incidents when Paul announced God's judgement to particular individuals.

1. Bar-Jesus the sorcerer and false prophet

In Acts 13:4–12, a sorcerer and false prophet called Bar-Jesus attempted to prevent Barnabas and Saul from speaking the word of God to the proconsul of Paphos. Saul looked Bar-Jesus full in the face and announced that he would be blind 'for a time'. Acts 13:9 underlines that Paul was 'filled with the Spirit' when he made this announcement, and 13:11 stresses that the blindness was the work of 'the hand of the Lord'.

It is important we grasp that Paul was not lashing out in temper at someone who was just being difficult. The sorcerer was actively preventing the proconsul from hearing the good news about Jesus, and so was an obstacle in the way of the kingdom. By opposing himself to the work of God in this way, Bar-Jesus placed himself under God's judgement. These are serious matters, and God judged him.

When the sorcerer was struck blind, the proconsul became a believer – because he was astonished by what he had learnt about the Lord. This incident shows that speaking with God's prophetic authority in this way is a significant 'breakthrough' ministry in evangelism.

2. Ananias the High Priest

In Acts 23:1–5, as Paul began to speak to the Sanhedrin, Ananias, the High Priest, ordered a servant to hit Paul on the mouth. In response, Paul announced that God would strike him.

It seems that Paul did not realise he was speaking to the High Priest, as he apologised when this was pointed out to him. Paul's quote from Exodus 22:28 shows, however, that he knew he was speaking something like a divine curse.

The fact that Paul apologised for breaking the Mosaic Law rather than for announcing God's judgement proves that Paul believed it was possible for believers to minister in this way. History records that, five years later, Ananias was assassinated while still in office – the only High Priest to die in this way in all Jewish history.

Other examples

There are many other biblical examples which show that God's servants are sometimes prompted to speak out or announce God's judgement. We should note that, in nearly all these examples, the words spoken were a curse or judgement against an individual – or group of people – who was hindering or opposing God's work.

- ◆ Noah cursed Canaan – Genesis 9:25–27.
- ◆ The ten plagues on Egypt were ten judgements which were prophetically announced by Moses and Aaron – Exodus 7–11.

- The seals, trumpets and bowls of plagues are prophetic judgements – Revelation 6; 8–9 & 15–16.
- Joshua cursed anyone who tried to rebuild Jericho – Joshua 6:26: the result, 500 years later, is seen in 1 Kings 16:34.
- Psalm 109 is probably a prophetic judgement on Judas by David.
- David cursed Joab and his descendants – 2 Samuel 3:26–32.

Jesus' spoken judgements

Mark 11:12–25 is an important passage about announcing God's judgement with God's prophetic authority. Jesus spoke to a tree which, because it had leaves, had all the appearance of bearing fruit, but had none in reality; he said, 'Let no one eat fruit from you ever again.'

The following day, the tree had dried up from the roots and died. The disciples betrayed no surprise at Jesus' words, only amazement at the speed with which they took effect. So Jesus taught them how to minister in the Spirit with his prophetic authority and effectiveness – just as he had taught them to pray, to minister healing and to cast out demons.

Jesus took the common Jewish phrase 'to move a mountain' and vested it with new power and application. This phrase is based in Isaiah 40:1–5, where the prophet was told to prepare the way of the Lord. Among other things, Isaiah had spiritually to knock down the mountains of difficulty which were obstructing the wide-spread revelation of the glory of God. 'Mountain-moving' is hinted at in Isaiah 2:11–16 and its counterpart of 'uprooting' is suggested in Lamentations 3:65–66. The idea also appears in Zechariah 4:7.

At a physical level, the phrase 'mountain-moving' was used when a king wanted to travel to distant parts of his kingdom. A party of men would be sent, some six months to a year in advance, to prepare the way for the royal party. These men would make good the bridges, repair the paths, uproot trees and generally do everything they could to 'move-mountains' to facilitate the easy journeying and swift arrival of the monarch.

Jesus took up the idea of spiritual mountain-moving from Isaiah, and developed it in three parallel passages: Matthew 17:20; Mark 11:22–24 & Luke 17:5–6. These passages show that, for Christ's disciples, speaking with Christ's prophetic authority means dealing with obstacles which are preventing God's glory from being seen, God's will from being done, and God's rule from being established.

We need to understand Mark 11:22 correctly. Most English translations suggest that Jesus said, 'Have faith *in* God'. But 'Have faith *of* God' is probably a better translation. We could even say, 'Have faith in God's faith'. We consider this in Part Five of *Living Faith*.

God's faith is absolute. He is totally self-confident. He knows that he can achieve whatever he wants to do. 'Mountain-moving' and 'up-rooting' are not a problem to Almighty God. When we have a speck of God's faith in us – or when we trust in his faith – it becomes much more straightforward to speak with Christ's authority in judgement against a person or situation which is blocking or resisting God's will.

Matthew 17:20 & Luke 17:5–6 show that we do not need much faith to move mountains or uproot obstacles, just the genuine article. It is quality, not quantity, that counts. On its own, our faith can achieve nothing – it is God who moves the mountains. Our faith merely engages us with the great power of God. We examine this more fully in the *Sword of the Spirit* volume *Living Faith*.

There seem to be five stages in speaking with God's authority against a spiritual obstacle or barrier.

1. Knowing God's will
We must never forget the Balaam principle that we cannot bless those whom God does not bless and that we cannot curse those whom God does not curse.

This means that we must spend time listening to the Spirit to receive his identification of any obstacles which are preventing God's glory from being seen or his will from being done – *and* which he wants us to his speak against. We need to learn from the Spirit what factors, people and attitudes are preventing the work of God from developing.

Matthew, Mark and Luke each imply an obstacle in their parallel passages on spiritual mountain-moving.

◆ Matthew suggests that difficulty in ejecting demons may require this ministry.

◆ Mark insinuates that personal relationships, especially those in which unforgiveness exists, can be a 'mountain' to be 'moved'. He also identifies the need for ministers to walk in forgiveness.

◆ Luke also hints that the stubborn roots of unforgiveness need to be uprooted.

2. Speaking God's command

These verses do not say, 'Whoever prays to me,' but, 'Whoever speaks to the mountain.' This ministry is not a prayer to the Father, it is a command spoken to the person or situation.

In practice, it is no different from the other examples we have seen of speaking, in the power of the Spirit, to eyes, limbs, demons and fevers, and commanding them 'in the name of Jesus' to be changed.

By now, we should have grasped that this is a key principle of all ministry in the Spirit. We often cry to God, 'Do something,' but the Spirit usually whispers back, 'No, you do it – in my power and in Jesus' holy name.' We must always remember that God is calling us into genuine partnership in ministry with the Spirit. He depends on our obedient words and actions, and we rely on his prompting and power.

3. Receiving God's faith

Home-produced faith is insufficient for this ministry. We need the God given confidence that our words will be effective. Paul knew that Elymas would be temporarily blinded. Peter was sure that Sapphira would drop dead.

The Holy Spirit's gift of his faith, referred to in I Corinthians 12:9, is very important for this ministry. We have seen that all ministry in the Spirit boils down to ministering the gifts of the Spirit, and that the gifts are aspects of the Spirit's own nature. When the Holy Spirit gives us the spiritual gift of some of his faith to help us in ministry, we really do have the faith that Jesus says we need in Mark 11:22. This means our words are charged with prophetic authority through the power of the Holy Spirit.

When the Spirit provides us with the gift of God's faith we are to accept the event as already being done. To believe in this way is not to have a faint hope that something could or might take place; for example, 'I think (but am not really sure) that Sapphira will die today.' Instead, to believe is to know for certain, for example, 'I believe (God has promised – and there is Ananias' body lying over there) that Sapphira will die today'.

4. Keeping on commanding
The Greek words used in Mark 11:23–24 mean that we are to 'go on saying' to the mountain, 'Get up and throw yourself into the sea.' It is not a one off command. We are to go on announcing God's judgement or order to a particular obstacle until it has been dealt with. This involves considerable patience and spiritual persistence.

5. Looking to a visible result
The construction of the phrases 'it will be done' and 'it will move', emphasises the certainty of fulfilment. Luke used a Greek word which referred to a time before the command, for example, 'it would have obeyed', and this underlines the fact that there is to be a visible consequence to our anointed words.

Ministering to people who have been cursed

We have seen that the Deuteronomy 27 curses do not apply to believers. And Galatians 3:13 shows that a central part of the gospel is the 'good news' that Christ has redeemed us from the curse of the Law so that we can enjoy the blessings of Abraham.

We must recognise, however, the futility of praying for sick people when they are affected by a curse. After David's curse in 2 Samuel 3:26–32, for example, it would be a waste of time praying for one of Joab's descendants to be healed of a discharging sore! They must be released from the curse before they are ministered to for healing.

We have also examined examples which show that, although God does not always curse us whenever we break some aspect of the Old Testament Law, he does judge some believers who become involved in habitual sin – but only to love them back to him.

God's loving chastening
Deuteronomy 28:15–68 lists the terrible ways that God cursed the people of Israel when they broke the Mosaic Law. These curses do not apply automatically to Christian believers; they do, however, point us towards the ways that God may, at times, chasten a believer.

There are six basic elements to Deuteronomy 28:

- ◆ Mental and physical sickness – verses 21, 22, 27, 28, 34 & 35
- ◆ Failure in every endeavour and enterprise – verses 25, 30 & 49
- ◆ Unavoidable poverty – verses 17, 18, 30, 31, 38 & 48
- ◆ Division and break-up – verses 30, 32 & 54
- ◆ Depression, sleep problems and binding fears – verses 65–67
- ◆ A sense of humiliation in the eyes of men and women, and of perpetual disfavour from God – verses 25, 37 & 68.

When we are ministering to a believer who seems to be experiencing many of the Deuteronomy 28 elements of chastening, we need to establish whether God is behind their difficulties.

We must not fall into the trap of thinking that every difficulty is the result of sin – in Christ, we have been set free from that sort of thinking. Some of our difficulties are the natural consequence of living in a fallen world which is still under the rule of the evil one. Other difficulties occur when we oppose and resist the evil one, and try to establish the rightful rule of God in the world. Not a few difficulties are due to our own foolishness, weakness and fleshly responses. Occasionally, however, a difficulty may be God's chastening. Clearly we need the Spirit's insight and discernment to recognise the root cause in each situation.

Release from God's chastening
Daniel 9:1–19 is a critical passage. When Daniel recognised that the people of Israel were under the judgement of God, he *repented personally* – with prayer and fasting – for his own sins and *confessed representatively* for his ancestors' sins. He did not confess only those sins that he had committed, but also the sins which had been committed by his family and nation.

Daniel wrestled in prayer with God, interceding for his mercy to be shown, for blessing, for the Lord to act without delay. The only way of release from God's judgement is by confession and repentance – with a firm promise of future obedience – and by pleading for God's mercy. We also see this in Ezra 9.

As representatives before God of their people, Daniel and Ezra confessed sins they had not personally committed. Families and churches which are under God's judgement for falling into sin in the past need to confess in a similar representative manner to make possible any lifting of God's chastening. However, it is important to notice that Daniel and Ezra did not, and indeed could not, repent for the sins of others. Representative confession does not involve representative *repentance*. No one can repent for the sins of another. But representative confession can (as the examples of

Daniel and Ezra imply) have an effect on God. It can lead to an outpouring of mercy and grace in which God brings repentance upon a people or an individual.

Any believer or group which is under the judgement of God can only throw themselves on his mercy and grace: there is no automatic release. We must not forget, however, that God is quick to bless all those who come to him in sincere repentance. If God is full of mercy, is merciful, it must mean that his mercy is infinite.

Demonically enforced curses

The Bible never specifically describes the consequences of curses enforced by Satan. The following suggestions, therefore, are based on experience rather than the Scriptures, and should not be given too much authority.

These 'evidences of a demonic curse' should be looked for in several members of a family or group – maybe across several generations – rather than in one individual. And we should look for much more than the mere existence of any one evidence. There is normally a persistent history of several evidences, and a broad pattern of evidences which go beyond a single person.

We might see, for example:

- A history of many repeated suicide attempts in several generations
- Repeated miscarriages, difficulties at menstruation or menopause; other problems
- Repeated acute sickness, both physical and mental, especially when there is no clear medical diagnosis; these often seem as if they are about to be healed, but there is probably a history of repeated disappointments, of many promised cures which did not work
- Frequent stays in mental hospitals; premature senility in many generations; a series of nervous breakdowns in one family

◆ A highly improbable rate of accidents

◆ A family history of marriage breakdowns, alienation, intense wranglings, unforgiveness and strife

◆ A family has, on paper, an ample income, but it never has enough money to support itself and is continually in debt and hardship; in theory, they should prosper yet they are always suffering considerable material adversity.

We should look for several of these evidences before considering the possibility of the existence of a demon-enforced curse. Sometimes it will be obvious – but careful questions usually need to be asked, the answers verified, advice sought from colleagues, and then the wisdom and knowledge of the Holy Spirit *must* be received before we can proceed with any ministry to release a person from a curse.

Releasing a cursed person

The first stage in helping a cursed person is to establish that they are cursed. Sometimes a sufferer will have been told that they are being cursed; at other times their experience will suggest this as a possibility. We always need the Spirit's insight, especially his gift of 'the discerning of spirits', to be sure that a demon is behind the difficulties.

If we ourselves are cursed (and, as believers increasingly confront the forces of darkness, this is likely to happen more often) the Scriptures make the correct action clear. It is to counter the curse with blessing.

David may have countered Goliath's curse with a stronger one, but that is the only exception: elsewhere the principle is plain. Judges 17:1–3; Psalm 109:28; Luke 6:28; Romans 12:14, 21 & 1 Corinthians 4:12 all stress that God's children overcome a curse with blessing.

The following suggestions are guidelines for the release of a person, family or church which is under a demon-enforced curse.

Before beginning, we must help the person to 'move' from the place where the curse is effective to the place where they can be protected and can receive God's blessing. The only basis for this exchange is the atoning death of Christ.

Unless people are 'in Christ', and have consciously claimed by faith the benefits of the cross, they cannot begin to be released from a curse. Ministry can begin only when the person is in Christ and in vital fellowship with a local church. The person should then be helped through these stages of release.

- ◆ There should be a real personal repentance, perhaps over a period of time, for the cause of the curse. The Bible, in Proverbs 26:2, says that a curse cannot alight without a cause. This may involve representative confession for the sins of other people in the family or group. And if it is the case that there is no 'cause' for the curse then that brings great confidence to pray the prayer of release.

- ◆ A confession of faith in Christ should follow which establishes that the sufferer is trusting only in Christ's work on the cross for their transfer from the place of curse to the place of blessing.

- ◆ A clear scriptural basis for release should be established. Some of the scriptural promises should be claimed: for example, Isaiah 14:12–19; Ezekiel 28:17–19; John 12:31; Galatians 3:13–14; Ephesians 1:7; Colossians 1:12–14; 1 John 3:8; Revelation 18 & Luke 10:17–19.

- ◆ Any contact with the evil one made by the sufferer, or by their immediate friends and family, should be renounced and revoked.

- ◆ All the relevant people should be forgiven, especially the person who uttered the curse and the one who caused the curse.

◆ Release should be announced by a person who is in a position of some spiritual authority over the sufferer: for example, the father, husband, elder or minister.

◆ They should address the evil spirit which is enforcing the curse and forbid it, in the name of Jesus, from bringing any further evil or harm upon the person or family. The demon should be told that the person is now protected by the name of God, and that – by the finished work of Christ upon the cross – the devilish curse is to be replaced with divine blessing.

◆ Hands should then be laid upon the sufferer and a blessing announced. If they have not been filled with Holy Spirit, that blessing should be sought.

Part Eleven

The ministry of counselling

We have seen the way that Jesus served or ministered to individual people through healing, deliverance and blessing. We also need to recognise that he also ministered by counselling or advising them. Although the Gospels record that much of Jesus' teaching was addressed generally to small groups and large crowds, it also describes many counselling encounters with particular individual people. Truly, he was the wonder-counsellor of Isaiah 9:6.

Although counselling is an important part of ministry in the Spirit, it differs in two important respects from the other types of ministry that we have examined.

♦ Healing, deliverance and blessing aim to meet people's needs for them. Amongst other things, counselling offers God's advice and direction; it passes on God's recommended course of action, for the people to follow themselves.

♦ Healing and deliverance bring about an immediate transformation; counselling establishes a long-term realignment with God's will.

Some people suppose that counselling takes place whenever believers give advice. But genuine counselling ministry occurs only when a follower of Jesus passes on God's will and purpose, for counselling is a conversation between God, the minister, and the person being helped.

Although 'counselling' is an important element of ministry in its own right, it is also the ongoing after-care which follows after deliverance and healing.

As we have seen, it is rarely adequate just to pray for a person's healing or deliverance, and then to leave them as we pass quickly on to someone else. We also need to ask God what he wants to say to the person, whether the person would benefit from divine counselling, and what they should do next to make spiritual progress.

Counselling and discipleship

In Part Three we saw that all ministry in the Spirit depends on discipleship, and that we need 'to learn' from Christ and follow his example in everything. Quite simply, counselling is discipling; it is helping a person to learn from Christ and to follow his example rather than their own ideas.

We also saw that ministry in the Spirit depends on our ability to listen to the Spirit and to test and recognise his promptings. Although this is true for all ministry, it is especially important in counselling.

If we follow our own thoughts and ideas when we try to minister healing to a person, the person may not be helped and healed but there are unlikely to be any long-term negative results. But if we pass on our own opinions while counselling, we are establishing a long-term realignment of the person's life with our will rather than with God's will — and that can have serious consequences.

All the material we consider in this section is completely based in Part Three, and should be studied in conjunction with that section. In fact, it is probably advisable to re-read Part Three before proceeding.

Counselling and the Word

Christian counselling uses the Scriptures as God's authoritative and sufficient manual for life and living, The Bible provides the counsellor with everything he needs to know about our relationship with God and our neighbour, as the following scriptures show: 2 Peter 1:3–4, 16–21; 2 Timothy 3:14–17 & Deuteronomy 29:29.

Counselling and the Spirit

We have seen that the prophets were the Old Testament counsellors – 2 Chronicles 25:5–16 & Jeremiah 38:14–28 illustrate this association. We can think of prophecy as 'the passing on of God's word', and counselling as 'the passing on of God's wisdom'. Any Old Testament Jew could give sensible advice, but only anointed prophets could pass on God's wisdom.

As we know, at Pentecost, prophesying, counselling, healing – all ministry in the Spirit – ceased to be the prerogative of a few special people. Now any believer who has been anointed with the Spirit can speak God's words, can minister in the Spirit, can counsel.

Christian counselling is impossible without the Holy Spirit. Christ promised his disciples the presence of the Holy Spirit or (the *Parakletos*) the 'one who is called alongside to assist'. The Holy Spirit as the Helper or Counsellor introduces the changes that God desires in the life of a Christian. The counsellor must rely on this dynamic for change at every stage of the counselling process.

All change that is not motivated by and performed in the power of the Holy Spirit is sub-Christian and fundamentally unpleasing to God.

The aim of Christian counselling is to see the counselee free from bondages, sinful practices and erroneous thinking, so that he or she grows in the fruit and gifts of the Holy Spirit.

Counselling and advice

We must distinguish good advice from God's counsel. Two Greek words represent these ideas. *Boule* is best translated as 'counsel' and means 'a declaration of the will of God', while *gnome* means 'advice' and refers to opinions based on reason, experience and knowledge.

In 1 Corinthians 7:25, Paul offered *gnome*, whereas in 1 Corinthians 14:37 he declared *boule*, even though the word *boule* is itself not used. The difference between the two is clear: in the latter, Paul knew that there was a clear command in

Christ's teaching which was relevant for every situation; but in the former, he was passing on his apostolic judgement about the specific situation in Corinth. We can say that Paul's advice in 7:25–40 was *gnome* to him, yet was to be received as *boule* in Corinth by virtue of his apostolic office.

This does not mean that human experience and common sense should be disregarded, merely that they must be complemented by a clear command from the Word – from Jesus or Scripture. Our experience may help us know 'how' to counsel, but only the Holy Spirit can tell us 'what' to say.

As well as the basic idea of 'giving advice' found in the use of *boule* in the New Testament, and its Hebrew counterpart *etsah*, there are other vitally important words which are relevant to the counselling process.

'Comfort and exhort'
- ◆ *Parakaleo* – 'called alongside to give help', 'to encourage', 'to comfort', 'to exhort' – for example, Romans 12:1; 2 Corinthians 1:4,6; Ephesians 6:22; Philippians 4:2 & 1 Thessalonians 4:18.

- ◆ *Paramutheomai* – 'to encourage', 'to console with speech' – John 11:19, 31, 1 Thessalonians 2:11 & 5:14.

'Admonish and warn'
- ◆ *Noutheteo* – 'to put in mind', 'to warn', 'to stimulate', 'to encourage positively' – Acts 20:31; Romans 15:14; 1 Corinthians 4:14; Colossians 1:28; 3:16; 1 Thessalonians 5:12, 14 & 2 Thessalonians 3:15. In the Greek version of the Old Testament, it is recorded that Eli remonstrated with his sons, 1 Samuel 2:24, but failed to admonish them, 1 Samuel 3:13.

'Correct and restore'
- ◆ *Elegcho* – 'to convict', 'to reprove', 'to rebuke' – John 16:8; 2 Timothy 4:2; Titus 2:15 & Revelation 3:19. This must not be confused with *epitimao*

which means simply 'to rebuke' (*epitimao* may be undeserved, Matthew 16:22, or may be ineffectual, Luke 23:40, but *elegcho* implies rebuke which brings conviction, John 8:46).

'Equip and make fit'
- ◆ *Katartizo* – 'to render fit', 'to mend', 'to repair', 'to restore' – Galatians 6:1. *Katartizo* is used of mending nets in Matthew 4:21 & Mark 1:19.

'Instruct and teach'
- ◆ *Paraggello* – 'to give word', 'to order', 'to command' – Mark 6:8; Luke 8:29; 9:21; Acts 5:28; 2 Thessalonians 3:4,6,10 & 12.

- ◆ *Didasko* – 'to teach', 'to give instruction' – Matthew 4:23; 9:35; Romans 12:7; 1 Corinthians 4:17; 1 Timothy 2:12 & 4:11

Counselling guidelines

This short word study suggests the following basic guidelines for counselling. It points us in the right direction and helps us to see how counselling relates to the other elements of ministry in the Spirit.

1. Ask God
2 Samuel 16:20–17:23 tells the story of Ahithophel. His description, in 16:23, should be the aim of every believer. The counsel we give should be received only by asking God in prayer and studying his Word.

2. Remember to encourage as well as to correct
The need to 'give advice' can be a trap for the counsellor who can forget to listen to the person's needs, and to empathise with them. Advice should only be given with sensitivity, when the person asks for it and when they are ready to hear it. It is easy to be judgemental and apply scriptures inappropriately, insensitively and superficially. This is not really counselling with the Spirit or the Mind of Christ.

3. Do not obscure God's will

There will be occasions when we are unsure of Christ's clear command. In these situations, we must make it plain that our words are only our opinion: we should not want the divine rebuke of Job 38:2.

Paul's admission, in 1 Corinthians 13:9, that the gift of prophesy was imperfect, suggests that we should exercise some 'holy hesitation' when we counsel. For example, 'I think this is what God is suggesting' is probably better than, 'This is what God says you must do.'

Of course, when the Scriptures relate directly to the person's situation, we should always stress that God's Word must be obeyed. But when our counsel is prophetic, we should remind people that our words must be tested carefully and received cautiously.

4. Remember that God's counsel can be rejected

John the Baptist was God's appointed and anointed counsellor in Luke 7:29–30. The counsel he had received from God and passed on to his listeners was that they should repent and be baptised, but this was rejected by the Pharisees.

Throughout the Bible, the prophets were rejected – even Jesus was arrested and crucified as a false prophet. Believers who follow in these anointed footsteps are bound to face some similar rejection.

5. When rejected, do not become depressed

If our counsel is ignored, we should not repeat Ahithophel's mistake in 2 Samuel 17:1–23 – after Hushai the Archite's advice had been followed in preference to his own.

Rejection is not an excuse for depression, it as an opportunity to feel as God feels and share in Christ's sufferings. We should minister only because God prompts us, not because people listen to what we say.

6. Add no extra thoughts

In Numbers 22:2–24:25, Balak put pressure on Balaam to curse the Israelites. But Balaam stood firm and, in 22:8, 18, 38;

23:12 & 24:13, made it clear that he had to restrict his counsel to whatever God said.

There are often temptations to add to, or alter God's revelation. These must be resisted. We must speak only what God suggests, and add no extra thoughts of our own.

7. Do not draw back

In Acts 20:27, Paul said that he had not shunned to declare God's whole counsel. *Hupostello* is a nautical Greek verb which means 'to lower a sail' and is best translated as 'slackening' or 'drawing back'.

Paul always spoke in 'fear and trembling', yet he did not draw back from declaring the *boule* of God. When ministering, we will sometimes think, 'I could never say that'. We must not draw back: if it is God's word it must be passed on – with an anointed prophet's spiritual authority and a domestic servant's natural humility.

8. Make it clear

Hebrew 6:17 shows that God used an oath because he wanted his counsel to be both sure and clear. Jesus used everyday parables to make his teaching simple and memorable. And we must ask God to help us to be similarly creative in our counselling.

Though we are called to repeat the Spirit's advice, we have to use our own personality, words, illustrations, examples and analogies. Our ministry will be ineffective if the person's understanding of God's counsel is different from our own.

When counselling, we must be clear and simple in all we say to ensure that there is no confusion about God's wisdom.

9. There will be varied consequences

God's counsel has many different intended results. We see this, for example, in Acts 2:23; Isaiah 23:8–9 & Psalm 32:8–11.

This means that we cannot choose to pass on only one aspect of God's wisdom. For example, counselling is not rebuking people when they make a mistake, it is gently pointing out God's path to life for them.

10. There should be definite results
Isaiah 14:24, 27; 46:10–11 & Ephesians 1:11 make it plain that God's words must have definite results.

God's will and purpose are all-powerful, and in time everything will conform to his *boule*. However, when we minister by counselling in the Spirit, we are often only 'sowing seeds' for the future. It is a mistake, therefore, to judge by immediate results. We should not forget that the Spirit will remind people of our words at a later time.

The divine counsellor

As with every aspect of ministry in the Spirit, we can counsel only by sharing with the Father, the Son and the Spirit in their work. Counselling is not something we should perform independently of God – with only a quick prayer for guidance.

Like all ministry in the Spirit, counselling is a God-initiated, God-shared task. This means that we should look to the Scriptures and examine God's own counselling activities to learn about his work.

The Father
Isaiah 28:29 & Job 12:13 present the Father as a wise and wonderful counsellor; and Genesis 26:24; Numbers 22:20; 1 Samuel 3; 15:16; 1 Kings 19; 2 Chronicles 1:7; 7:12; Daniel 7; Acts 16:9 & 18:9 describe his ministry to particular men and women.

Genesis 16:13; 1 Samuel 2:3 & Jeremiah 32:18–20 show that God sees and knows everything – and he never leaves us in darkness when we are ministering in the Spirit.

He sees what the person's real problem is and knows what caused their difficulty. Nothing is hidden from him, and he will do for us what he did for Balaam in Numbers 24:16. He will often reveal a small part of his knowledge to us so that we know what he knows about a matter.

If we have been anointed with the Spirit, it is important that we trust those ideas which come into our minds while counselling. They may seem foolish, but they can be God's wisdom. Effective counselling, like all ministry in the Spirit, hinges on our ability to recognise the word and the wisdom of God.

Psalm 119:24 shows that the Father uses Scripture in his counselling ministry, and his written word is extremely important in counselling.

The Son

Isaiah 9:6 prophetically describes a child yet to be born: That child was Jesus, and all these titles belong to him: he is the Wonder-Counsellor.

The Scriptures present a well-rounded picture of Jesus' counselling ministry. For example, Jesus:

- ◆ Patiently explains the Scriptures to Cleopas and his companion – Luke 24:13–25
- ◆ Politely rebukes a disgruntled Martha – Luke 10:38:42
- ◆ Exudes discretion, compassion, courtesy, forgiveness and moral integrity when speaking to an adulterous woman – John 8:1–11
- ◆ Is firm and uncompromising when dealing with the rich young ruler – Mark 10:17–22
- ◆ Brings exposure, acceptance, joy and salvation to a corrupt official – Luke 19:1–10
- ◆ Patiently listens to the fearful ramblings of a sick woman, and then ministers health and peace into her life – Luke 8:43–48.

The Spirit

Isaiah 11:2 is an important description of the Holy Spirit which shows that counsel is basic to the Spirit's nature. In John 14:16, Jesus described the Spirit as *allos parakletos*. These Greek words show that:

- ◆ The Spirit is another counsellor who is the same type as Jesus
- ◆ The Spirit is called alongside us, to call to us and to call for us.

He is a counsellor who is both near and intimate, whose counselling is a gentle whispering in the human ear. This means that, if we are to share with the Spirit in his work, we must also get alongside those we are helping, and must depend at all times on the Spirit's promptings.

The Spirit is so self-effacing that he has recorded few examples of his counselling. Acts 10 is probably the clearest example.

First, the Spirit prepared the way by sending an angelic messenger to Cornelius, instructing him to send for 'a man called Simon, known as Peter'. (This shows that our ministry is usually just one small piece in the Spirit's grand design for each person.)

Then the Spirit picked his moment carefully. He waited until Peter was wanting to pray but too hungry to pray properly. He placed a picture into Peter's mind and ordered Peter to kill and eat animals that Jews were forbidden even to touch.

Finally, the Spirit repeated this command three times, fully aware how meaningful this three-fold repetition would be to Peter – John 18:27 & John 21:15–19.

When Cornelius' men arrived, Peter was too confused to hear their calls, so the Spirit told Peter about them and instructed him to return with them. This time Peter obeyed, and gradually realised the deep significance of the picture that the Spirit had planted in his mind.

This counselling ministry changed the course of the church. The Spirit had not argued with Peter; he had gently pressed his point, with the aid of the surrounding circumstances, until Peter realised the divine origin and revolutionary meaning of the Spirit's words and pictures.

The basis of counselling

The New Testament states seven times that the Old Testament Law can be reduced to two simple precepts: 'Love the Lord your God with all your heart, mind and strength' and 'Love your neighbour as yourself'.

I John 4:8 teaches that God is love; I John 3:9–10 promises that his children will reproduce his love; and John 13:34 commands us to love other disciples in the same way as Jesus has loved us.

This love is the basis of all counselling – and of all ministry – in the Spirit. We counsel because we love, because we have been filled and changed by God's love. The New Testament suggests many implications of this loving which are important for counselling ministry.

Love obeys

John 14 weaves together love, obedience and the Counselling Spirit. Loving obedience to Christ is the only sure basis for all our counselling: we should do only what he says, go only where he sends, and speak only what he suggests.

We have seen that the biblical initiative for ministry was always either a human request or a divine instruction. This is also true for counselling. The prophets passed on God's wisdom when an individual requested counsel, for example, I Kings 22:5–28 & 2 Kings 3:11–20; and when God sent them to deliver his counsel, for example, 2 Samuel 12:1–15 & I Kings 20:13–14. Occasionally, as in I Kings 14:1–18, they were both sought and sent.

Jesus repeated this pattern. In John 3:1–21 & Mark 10:17–22, he counselled people when they came for advice; and, in Luke 7:36–49 & 24:13–32, he went to people to pass on God's counsel to them.

Love gives

John 3:16 & 3:35 demonstrate that God is a loving giver, and Ephesians 5:2 & I John 4:10–11 link his loving and giving. God's love means generous actions, not just kind words. This means that we are often called to give in many practical ways when we minister.

We are called to give ourselves, to spend and be spent sacrificially in the service of others. We see this in Matthew 5:42; John 15:13; Romans 5:8; 2 Corinthians 8:7–9, 24; 12:15 & I John 3:16.

Love prays
One of the most important things that we can do for the people we serve is to pray for them. Roman 8:34–35 & Hebrews 7:25 show that the Wonder-Counsellor intercedes for his friends; and, in Romans 15:30, Paul insists that his readers will pray for him if they love him.

Love speaks the truth
Mark 10:21 reports that Jesus looked at a man and loved him, and this love meant that Jesus spoke a very hard truth. We can speak God's truth truthfully only when we love as Christ loves, because our counsel ceases to be God's type of truth when it is not initiated and saturated by his love. As in Mark 10:22–23, God's loving, truthful words carry no guarantee of acceptance.

How can this love be possible for a believer? The demands of 1 Corinthians 13 seem hopelessly unattainable. When we are ministering, we find that people, situations and problems repeatedly expose our lack of love.

Whenever we ask the question, 'How?' the biblical answer is always the same: 'The Holy Spirit: he will come upon you.' In John 17:26, Jesus prayed that the love of the Father, who loved the Son, would fill us. He did not pray for our love to be increased, but for it to be replaced by the Father's love.

2 Timothy 1:7 teaches that God's gift is a spirit of love, and Romans 5:5 points to this love-filling work of the Spirit. When our ministry really is 'in the Spirit', we will find that we are motivated and empowered by the Father's love.

Basic counselling equipment

The Bible is the counsellor's text book. If counselling in the Spirit is meant to help people bring their lives into harmony with God's Word, the counsellor must know, and know well, the Scriptures.

Many different books are available which apportion different sections of the Bible to various human problems. These are helpful, but they are second best to an intimate personal acquaintance with the Bible.

The Scriptures are relevant to every problem, situation and need.

- ◆ There is a Psalm for every emotion and every situation, and the book of Psalms has been the mainspring of Christian worship for centuries. Yet it is now almost unknown in some church traditions.

- ◆ Ephesians can be considered the gospel of unity. It reveals God's way forward for troubled relationships and contains his recipe for spiritual survival in times of conflict.

- ◆ Proverbs is rarely read in public worship or private devotion, yet it contains crystallised counselling material.

- ◆ The Sermon on the Mount, Matthew 5–7, describes the way Jesus expects his followers to live. It is full of God's practical advice.

- ◆ Romans 8 is, for many people, the climax of the Bible. It contains assurance, direction, comfort, encouragement and hope.

We should read the Bible regularly, frequently, carefully and fully. We must saturate ourselves in the Gospels so that we know Jesus better; and we should not neglect the forgotten books like Leviticus and Obadiah; Lamentations and Zephaniah; 2 Chronicles and Nahum.

Who knows? Maybe, someday, the Spirit will prompt us to use a verse from these one of these books to counsel a person. And think how embarrassing it will be if we meet Habakkuk in heaven and have to admit that we cannot spell his name and have never read his book!

When using the Scriptures in ministry, we must watch that we do not always use the same favourite passage. Jesus only used John 3:16 when he counselled Nicodemus, not with every person he advised.

The gifts and attributes of the Spirit
Like all ministry, counselling in the Spirit revolves around the gifts and attributes of the Spirit. We looked at these earlier and they are also considered in *Knowing the Spirit*.

These gifts, 1 Corinthians 12:1–11, and attributes, Isaiah 11:1–5, are not an ability to do something, they are the work of the Lord Jesus through us. They are the energy and person of the Spirit, not the activity of a believer.

In 1 Corinthians 12:7, the Greek verb *didomi*, 'to give', appears in a form which suggests that:

- ◆ God's giving of gifts to believers is a continuous activity, not a once-for-all action
- ◆ Each person receives the gifts from an outside source, from the Holy Spirit.

This means that, when a gift is manifested, believers do not dig into their personal resources, they pass on what they have just received from the Spirit. As we live in and with the Spirit, so he gives us everything that we need for every ministry situation as it arises.

Isaiah 11:3–4 shows that the attributes of the Spirit in 11:2 have a particular application in counselling. These attributes are not gifts which are regularly given, they are the very essence of the Spirit's being which naturally flows from those in whom he lives.

This means that, as we live in and with him, his attributes are continually available to us. Whenever we counsel in the Spirit, his own wisdom and understanding, his personal counsel and insight, can flow through us to the people we are serving.

The counselling objective

At times, effective counselling means just listening to someone pour out their troubles. On other occasions, we need to talk with a person for only a short while – after that, God requires no more. But, more commonly, God calls us to counsel people over a longer period of time. In such cases, the ministry can deteriorate into aimless chit-chat unless God's objective for the person is understood and kept in mind.

The aim of Christian counselling should always be to bring about a long-term realignment with God's will. When preparing to meet with a person, it is easy to think 'How am I going to sort out this problem?' Such thinking often leads to glib answers. It is usually better to ask 'How does God want to use this situation to prepare the person for more effective service?'

Perhaps the best scriptural example of longer-term counselling ministry is Jesus' preparation of Peter for service.

Jesus counselling Peter
The story of this anointed ministry is reported in: John 1:40–42; Mark 1:16–20; Luke 5:1–11; Mark 3:13–19; Matthew 14:22–33; 16:13–23; Mark 9:2–13; Matthew 18:21–22; 19:27–30; John 13:2–10; Matthew 26:30–35; John 18:10–11; Mark 16:7; Luke 24:34; 1 Corinthians 15:1–5 & John 21:1–23.

During three years of patient counselling by Jesus, Peter was transformed from an impetuous, unreliable Simon into a dependable Peter who took the initiative in the replacement of Judas, was pre-eminent at Pentecost, and temporary leader of the church until the emergence of James and Paul.

It seems that Jesus had a clear objective in mind as he befriended, trained and counselled Peter. Simon was to become Peter; he was to be characterised by a rock-like resolution and reliability; he was to be and become a fisher of men.

Jesus did not keep this Spirit-given knowledge to himself. He told Peter from the outset what God wanted to accomplish through their companionship. Jesus made sure that Peter knew the counselling goal.

We must recognise that Jesus did not attempt to transform Peter by instant ministry. He did not lay hands on him. He did not attempt to cast out a spirit of unreliability and impetuosity.

He did not even bless him by prophetically announcing, 'Be filled with rock-like strength'. Instead, Jesus refined Peter slowly by patient, anointed counsel.

When Peter first started to follow Jesus, he brought with him his background, his vices, his mistakes, prejudices, wrong ideas, family problems and false self-confidence. Our first ministry objective should be to teach people to die – to die to the world, the flesh and the devil.

Jesus did not announce his Messiahship; instead he urged Peter to draw his own conclusions. When Peter got it right, Jesus pricked his pride by saying that he had not worked it out himself. Almost immediately, Jesus then rebuked Peter for remonstrating with him.

Peter was not 'possessed' by an evil spirit, he had merely listened to the whisperings of Satan. If the counselling objective was to be achieved, and Peter was to become an effective fisher of men, he had to learn the difference between the Father's voice and the enemy's. Jesus was counselling him to understand and appreciate the difference.

Intercession is vital if the objective is to be attained. Luke 22:32 reveals Jesus as having already prayed and listened and been enabled to bring a prophetic message – Peter will fall, recover and strengthen others.

Jesus did not condemn Peter as a conceited fool who ought to have known better, instead he allowed Peter to come to terms with himself – to perceive himself as he really was.

In counselling we should not criticise mistakes, nor place a protective cocoon around the person. Rather, we should point them to Jesus and help them to hear his voice and seek his face for themselves.

After his denial, Peter became despondent. So, before visiting the other disciples, Jesus met with him privately. What precious words of forgiveness and delight must have been exchanged! As counsellors we must be quick to make contact and offer forgiveness when the person we are helping feels that they have betrayed us or let us down.

Despite this, Peter returned to his old haunts and habits. So God arranged a fishing failure and the repetition of a miracle from the days when Peter was first called to follow Christ. Again, Peter was being counselled that there could be success only with Jesus in full control.

The final ministry session took place over breakfast. Jesus questioned Peter three times to clear away any doubt on the issue, thus recalling Peter's threefold denial and, as it were, putting each one to death. Jesus was about to leave the world and had to leave his sheep in capable hands. He had already called Peter to be a fisher of men, and now Peter was given another task: he was to work by hook and by crook. The objective was in sight, so the calling was clarified.

The objective of counselling is not merely to solve a problem, but to present a person as mature in Christ. This can mean a considerable commitment to the person's care. Jesus often talked with Peter during their time together, and this is an example of the long-term commitment which can be involved in counselling ministry.

Even at the end of this time, Peter still needed correction. When he asked about John, Jesus had to tell Peter that it was none of his business. Peter was a slow learner; he had to press on, and, having been counselled by Christ, he did press on right to the end.

Peter become the apostles' spokesman at Pentecost, and was imprisoned after healing a lame man. He performed more cures and was imprisoned again. He spoke boldly before magistrates, introduced the Holy Spirit to the Samaritans, and confounded Simon Magus.

Peter cured Aeneas, resuscitated Tabitha, and announced salvation to the Gentiles. He was imprisoned a third time; he opposed Paul, then commended his letters. He wrote two letters of his own, and finally, tradition asserts, died a martyr's death – crucified upside down because he believed that he was unfit to die in the same position as Jesus.

Throughout those three years of patient counsel, Jesus always held this vision of Peter's useful service before him. Whatever the problem, no matter what the defects and limitations of the person, we must ask God for his objective in the counsel.

When we are ministering, we should also ask for a vision of the person's useful service to pray for and work towards. Only by patient, anointed counsel can the Peters around us be rescued from the misery of rejection, failure and self-condemnation, be gently restored, and then be made ready for effective and useful service in the kingdom of God.

Starting to minister God's counsel

For many believers, counselling has been the 'way in' to ministry in the Spirit. They are nervous about being involved in the obviously supernatural aspects of ministry like healing and casting out demons, but are less apprehensive about counselling. Through learning to listen to the Spirit before counselling, however, and through relying on his gifts and words in counselling, they develop the confidence and expertise in the Spirit to move out in areas like healing and deliverance.

The best place to begin is by praying for our friends, neighbours, relatives and the fellow members of our local church. We have seen that it is helpful to develop the habit of asking God questions. We can, for example, ask him, 'Is there anyone you need me to visit and counsel?' or, 'Is there anything I should mention to John when I have lunch with him tomorrow?'

God takes such prayers very seriously – especially when we have been filled with the Spirit and have made ourselves available for humble ministry in the same way as a first-century house-servant.

The following suggestions are for those who are inexperienced in counselling and want to get started. They are *gnome* rather than *boule*!

Confidentiality

People should be given an assurance that everything they say will remain confidential. Ministers should not normally repeat anything without their permission. If a counsellor normally shares deeply with their spouse, this should be made clear at the outset.

Notes

We do not need to take notes when we casually counsel a friend. Notes are only necessary when we are involved with a large number of people, and when we find it difficult to remember what he we have said to any one person.

We should always ask permission before we take notes, and should explain why we are doing this. It is usually more useful to note the advice that we give, and any impressions we received from God, than only what the person says.

Length

Several short sessions are usually more helpful than one long session. This allows for reflection on the counsel, and for the Holy Spirit to underline it by some other means.

Dependence

A careful balance needs to be maintained between encouraging people not to turn to other counsellors for different advice, and not causing the person to depend too much on the original minister.

Some counsellors become very intense with the people they are seeking to serve. This should be avoided as human pressure militates against the Spirit's work. We cannot live other people's lives, solve their problems or take their decisions.

We can, however, help them to take responsibility for their own actions, and teach them to listen to God for themselves so that they can stop depending on us and become someone who ministers to others.

Prayer

In the ministries of healing, deliverance and blessing, prayer is vital beforehand, but less important during the actual time of ministry. Prayer, however, must pervade the entire counselling relationship, and should be offered before, during and after the time of ministry.

Whenever uncertainty emerges, the counsellor should pause for prayer. The people being helped should always be encouraged to pray about their problems: those who find it difficult or unnatural to pray out loud or spontaneously can be given written prayers to use.

At times, prayer in tongues is most helpful. Again, we should explain to the person what we are doing before we pray in tongues with them.

Partnership

We have seen that partnership is a general principle of scriptural ministry, yet it may often be necessary to counsel alone. Only foolish believers, however, counsel members of the opposite sex on their own.

It is even less helpful to counsel without the knowledge and prayerful support of the local church. The leaders have a general pastoral responsibility for all the members and should know who is helping whom, even if they do not need to know all the details.

Ministry in the Spirit

We have seen that the work of ministry in the Spirit is so important that all church leaders are meant to busy themselves preparing the saints for ministry. Almighty God wants a vast number of believers who are willing to become his prophetic ministers – to be his humble servants who will do anything for him, anywhere, at any time.

Churches are full of people with problems, people who are praying and waiting, not for heavy dictatorship, but for humble service. They need someone who will listen and still love them;

someone who will share their troubles not censure their misdeeds; someone who will offer God's word, not impose a human opinion; someone who will come alongside and give their undivided attention; someone who will pray fervently, give generously and love sacrificially. They need to hear God's counsel. And God wants us to be ready and able to pass it on.

The world around us is full of hurting people who need to experience God's healing power, who need to be set free from the grip of evil, who need their miserable cursed situation to be replaced with God's blessing. They need someone who has been redeemed and filled with God's Spirit; someone who is willing sacrificially to 'go the extra mile'; someone who is not afraid to look ridiculous, who will speak God's words and carry out God's actions.

They need someone who will minister only in the Spirit – and God wants us to be just such a minister, and to train ever more ministers, so that his loving kingdom extends throughout our nations and reaches to the ends of the earth.